I

Parenting That Makes Cents

The Secret to Raising Financially Savvy Kids

Parenting That Makes Cents

The Secret to Raising Financially Savvy Kids

Father and daughter
Mike and Sabrina Raber

Published by Centsible Publishing Inc.
Milwaukee Wisconsin USA

Parenting That Makes Cents

The secret to raising financial savvy kids

Published by Centsible Publishing Inc.
Milwaukee Wisconsin USA

ISBN - 978-1-7334410-1-8 Paperback

Cover Design by:
Theresa Wilmot - Wilmot Designs
Kristal Young – Kristal Clear Graphics

Ordering information
To order additional copies, call us at 414-559-7535 or email us at Sabrina@childrenandbeyond.com

Dedication

We dedicate this book to Jennifer Raber, for being such a loving and supportive mother and wife; and to Monica and Sam, for being amazing children and siblings who also helped with the creation of this book.

Table of Contents

Acknowledgements

My daughter Sabrina and I would like to thank the many people over the years who have helped us to come up with many great stories and examples, and who have mentored us along the way.

The creation of this book is the culmination of a lifelong dream to go out and positively impact people's lives by empower- ing them to live a purpose-driven life. It is the first of many forthcoming resources geared toward helping families develop a strong financial foundation.

As we continued to develop and bring our dream into reality, we received the generous support of many great mentors. They helped keep us on track when we lost faith or focus. They helped to shape the man and father that I have become.

There are many people I would like to thank, starting with my own family for teaching me that I can do anything I set my mind to. That belief gave me the strength to continue when many of the people around me told me I was crazy for having such a dream.

My gratitude also goes to Sister Allen, who, when I was at a point in my life when I felt alone and lost, Sister Allen took me under her wing and helped rekindle an internal flame that had burned out. For that, she will always have a special place in my heart.

Sabrina and I would also like to give a special thanks to Brian Buffini and everyone at Buffini and Company. Without their help over the years, we would probably have lost our business, and perhaps worse. Brian, you and Joe Neigo have been both coaches and mentors, and we are proud to be able to call you friends. Because of all your help over the years, we have been able to teach hundreds of children how to save, share, and spend their money wisely. It is from all your teachings that we were able to write this book. We will be forever grateful.

Mike and Sabrina Raber
Milwaukee, Wisconsin October 2020

SECTION ONE:

THE BEGINNING

We attract into our lives whatever we give our energy, focus, and attention to, whether wanted or unwanted.
—Michael J Lasier

CHAPTER 1:
INTRODUCTION

All great things must start with a first step!

Sabrina

Hi, my name is Sabrina. My sister and brother are Monica and Sam, and our parents are Mike and Jennifer. I'm now 18 years old. When I was younger, I was what most people would call "different." Instead of playing with Barbie dolls, I played with basketballs. Instead of jamming to pop music, I listened to classical. But above all, instead of spending my money freely, I knew the secret about the evils of money and that I needed to spend money wisely.

I learned a lot about money from the many stories my father told us about clients and the financial mistakes they made. When I was eight years old, my father decided to take me along with him to different business conferences. For the next two years, I went to the same conference, and each year, the speaker, Brian Buffini, preached the same thing: financial reform, over and over again.

I found myself wondering how so many adults found themselves in financial difficulty. Being eight, I didn't understand the complexities of money in the same way I know about them today. But I did know the way people were handling money was not right. I could see my friends spending their nickels and dimes on candy and toys. It hit me.

These kids, my friends, would end up in the same situation as their economically desolate parents if they continued to spend their money this way.

Learning from the conferences, I saw the far-reaching effects of debt, and was terrified that my friends would experience the same challenges. One day, on the playground, I realized what I had to do. Armed with markers and paper, my stuffed dog, and an idea, I devised a plan to change the world.

With the help of my father and an artist friend, who had created a hexagonal piggy bank with different sections. I designed a business that would teach money management skills to children.

I had my start. I used the lessons I learned from Brian Buffini and even though it took me a long time to understand, I changed his words into simple methods my friends could learn. My plan was set. I would teach them about money and hope they could escape the pain I saw my own parents go through with every late bill, every credit card statement. After long thought, I named my business Children and Beyond. It was at that point where this book truly starts.

Within the year, I became "famous." Brian Buffini invited me to speak at his seminars. At the age of eight, I spoke in front of 1000 people; when I was nine, it was 1,500. I was nicknamed "The Money Girl," and my concept soon began to enter every one of Brian's workbooks. My first TV interview took place when I was almost ten on KOMO 7 News in Seattle, Washington, where we were living at the time. I wore a rainbow sweater and stared at the ceiling because I was so nervous.

The second TV interview took place in Portland, Oregon six months later. I was ready that time. 1

As I got older, I found it more and more difficult to be "The Money Girl." Friends drifted away, my family moved, I got involved in sports and music and school, and at times, found myself too busy to even think. But amidst all the activities lay the seed of the business I had started as an eight-year-old. I continued to carry with me the desire to make a difference, to help my friends, and to help children everywhere.

I realized that my seemingly insignificant idea was on track to save kids from growing up to be the same drowning-in-debt adults I sat next to every year at the conference. Somehow, I knew any changes needed to start with the parents. If the parents understood how to save, spend, and share their money the right way, their children would grow up able to pay for student loans, buy a house, and live a financially free life without worry. It was the exact thing I wanted those many years ago.

My father and I teamed up to bring this message to you. Our knowledge, our passion to help, is now in your hands. I hope this book is able to help all the kids I was unable to help, because I know these lessons can change the world, one child at a time.

Sabrina Raber

Mike Raber, Sabrina's dad

I saw a need and set out to fill it!
I saw a solution and set out to find it!
I had a vision and set out to create it!
—Mike Raber, age 12

When Sabrina and I began to talk about writing this book, we discussed the different aspects of becoming financially independent. In addition, we explored what we thought were the critical issues that parents, and through them, their children, needed to learn. We then came up with the following topics:

- Why it's important for kids to learn about money
- Why it's important to acquire a millionaire's mind set, and what that means.
- Why it's important for parents to have a budget and net worth statement and the steps that go into creating these documents.
- Why it's important for parents to have a detailed money management system and how to create one.
- Why it's important for parents to have a debt reduction and savings/investing plan
- Why it's important to set proactive, reachable goals
- Why it's important for kids to develop the discipline and patience needed to create wealth
- Why it's important for kids to learn how to overcome adversity
- Why it's important for kids to have different ways to generate income

For Sabrina, this book is a way for her to make a difference in other kid's lives. For me, it's the opportunity to share many of the lessons I have learned about perseverance and money and pass those experiences on to other parents which are on their own journey towards financial freedom. It is my goal to empower other parents to raise financially savvy kids, and in the process, hopefully avoid a lot of the financial mistakes that my wife Jennifer and I made along our own journey.

Sabrina and I will share many stories throughout this book, illustrating the benefits that come from teaching children the importance of overcoming challenges, developing an entrepreneur's mindset, setting goals while staying faithful through the process, giving to those less fortunate, and saving up for things we want. We hope these stories will inspire you to work toward bringing your own dreams and the dreams of your children into realty.

I would say one of the biggest lessons I would share with our kids while they were growing up, is one I learned early on. If your dream is big enough and if you have faith, in time you will be given the help needed to accomplish your dream. No matter how much adversity you may experience, or how much you might want to give up, if you stay focused on your dream, you will have the strength to overcome any challenges.

The benefits that came with having money became very clear to me. The more financially better off a person was, the more doors would be opened. I also realized that the amount of money people need varies for everyone and depends on their goals and the type of lifestyle they want to live.

As a youngster, I also learned if a person could learn to push past pain, push past fear, push past one's own self-doubt, in the end, you became stronger for it. Most importantly, I learned it was okay to dream, because even if things didn't turn out the way you had pictured, they would still be better than before.

There is nothing more
powerful than the
dream of a child!

CHAPTER 2:
THE BIRTH OF A DREAM

Teach Our Children Well

It became evident to me that if our goals and dreams are clear, and we don't let life sidetrack us, anything is possible. True victory is shown by winning a championship. However, that prize is earned through all the blood, sweat, and tears that led up to the victory.

As parents or people who have the ability to influence children, the better we are at setting goals, and managing our own money, the better example we will be to those around us. Most importantly, we need to make sure that we have a healthy mindset when it comes to money and finances. Sabrina's and my goal and dream is for parents to learn to raise future generations of children who are not only fiscally responsible, but also willing to help the world around them.

Granted, there were days I wanted to crawl under some rock and die—like all young people growing up. However, I knew that if I made it a lifelong goal to surround myself with others who shared similar values and to search out the right mentors, I would be able to help a lot of other people along the way. Who knew that three such mentors would be my three children?

I'll never forget the time when Sabrina came home from school. She was in second grade and seemed troubled. I asked her what was wrong, and she told me that she had watched one of her friends take a bunch of change out of her pocket and use it to buy candy at lunch.

I asked Sabrina if she felt that her friend shouldn't have bought the candy.

Sabrina responded, "No, it's not that I don't think she should have bought the candy. What bothers me is that the change clearly didn't have any value to her. It's not like she took a handful of change out of her pocket, chose a few coins to buy the candy, then put the rest back into her pocket. She took all the change out of her pocket and gave it all to the sales lady as if it didn't have any value."

Sabrina then told me that she started to think about stories I've told about different clients I've had, and she started to think that if we don't teach kids the value of money and how to properly manage it, they would end up broke and in financial trouble, like many of my clients were, when they grew up. I asked Sabrina what she wanted to do to help ensure that this didn't occur. Thus was born Children and Beyond.

Sabrina has since set out to help teach other kids money management skills. That way, they could grow up and not have to worry about money. Sabrina's company teaches kids money management habits and does workshops for kids with the hope of empowering kids so that they won't have to worry about money as they get older.

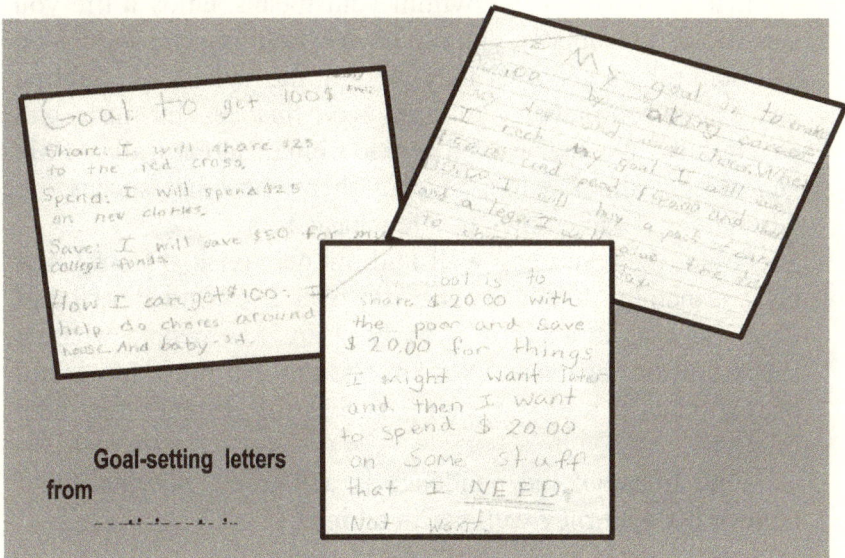

Goal-setting letters from

Sabrina and I believe it's very important to teach children about proper money management. However, we have found that many parents also need to acquire these skills. We would like to arm parents with the financial systems and tools necessary to create a stable and fiscally responsible environment in which to raise their kids.

Some of my own money lessons came from many years of listening to my family talk about money and politics. I learned some things from my stepfather, other lessons living with my dad, and even more by starting different businesses as a kid. Working in the restaurant and at many other jobs taught me many lessons.

As a consultant, I have also worked with clients from all different walks of life, and in many cases, while some appear to be well off, they are scrambling to "keep up with the Joneses." Joe Niego, a friend of ours in Chicago, often says, "People spend money they don't have, to buy things they don't need, to impress people they don't know." If you ask us, that's a goofy way to live. Said another way, "Money without sound values becomes impotent."

Instead, why not live within your means, enjoy a life you can afford, so that later, you can have everything you want. You can help others get what they want at the same time. Sabrina and I have continued to study money, finances, business, and psychology. We interviewed people from different walks of life and asked them what helped them become successful. Ultimately, it came down to a few basic things.

Success is the result of a well-laid-out plan created from a few basic principles practiced every day over an extended period of time. Success is a group activity. Very few people become successful on their own. We have found that most successful people relate that they became successful through the help of others.

True financial independence is a journey. Sabrina and I believe it's a journey well worth taking.

When it comes to money,
if kids can discipline
themselves to do the things
they need to do now, the day
will come when they can do
the things they want to do
when they want
to do them.
–Zig Ziglar

CHAPTER 3:
THE PATH TO FINANCIAL INDEPENDENCE

Why should kids learn about money?

Mike

My kids went to school to get a basic education, then came home to learn about business and finances. When they were small, I was determined to make
sure they grew up learning about money and how to properly manage it. Financial management is an ongoing process, and the more we stay disciplined to our plan, the faster we will see our dreams and goals start to come true.

As parents, when we set out to teach our kids about money and how to manage it, there are many different parts we need to explore. We need to talk about what money means or represents and show our children the difference between a need and a want. We can explore the different types of money, and how these are used. Depending on the age of the child, we may want to start with a simple explanation of what money is, or we may want to go into a lot more detail

Throughout this book, we will explore a detailed money management system for teaching children young or old important financial concepts around how to save, spend, and share the money they get. Whether they get money from gifts, doing odd jobs, or an allowance, the system will remain the same.

Sabrina and I have found that over the years of working with different clients and doing various seminars, parents and their children tend to have some common questions, such as:

✓ What are the different ways a kid can raise money?

✓ If I'm only ten, can I get a job?

✓ At what age should I start giving my child an allowance?

✓ Should I give my child an allowance?

✓ How much should I give my child for an allowance?

✓ Is it okay to pay my kids for doing chores around the house?

✓ I own a business. Should I put my kids on payroll?

✓ I can't even manage my own money; how am I supposed to teach my children how to manage theirs?

The list goes on. We will cover these questions and many more before we reach the end of this book.

When I sit down with people, I often hear them say things like, "I don't have very much money, so why do I need to worry about managing it now?" Or, "I know I should pay myself first, and I will, I just need to make a little more so I can do that." Or, my least favorite, "I don't need that much money to get by." True, but what if you had the ability to make more money than you needed? How many great causes or people would you be able to help? If we can do something to help others and we don't do it, we are not only cheating them, we are cheating ourselves as well.

By the time he or she graduates, the average high school senior will have learned many important life skills, yet the ability to manage money most likely will not be one of them. In fact, average high school seniors can't even balance a check book, let alone manage their money. They then go on to college and by the time they graduate from college, they often have high student loans and credit card debt. That's why people need to learn core financial management skills while they are still young.

If they wait until they are older to acquire these skills, it may be too late. If schools aren't teaching kids about money and how to manage it, where will they learn those skills? Certain things are better taught at home, money skills being one of them. After all, in most cases, who better to teach kids these skills than their parents?

There's one small problem with this kind of thinking. Who taught the parents about money and how to manage it? Society assumes that most parents have learned these skills, and then wonders why history repeats itself.

Sabrina and I believe it's time to put a halt to that assumption and start from the grassroots up.

Parents often spend years teaching their kids about the "birds and the bees," but neglect to discuss the subject of money. Some of the most important subjects on personal development, such as financial management and parenting skills, are generally not taught. In fact, parents are often expected to learn by trial and needed? How many great causes or people would you be able to help? If we can do something to help others and we don't do it, we are not only cheating them, we are cheating ourselves as well.

By the time he or she graduates, the average high school senior will have learned many important life skills, yet the ability to manage money most likely will not be one of them. In fact, average high school seniors can't even balance a check book, let alone manage their money. They then go on to college and by the time they graduate from college, they often have high student loans and credit card debt. That's why people need to learn core financial management skills while they are still young.

If they wait until they are older to acquire these skills, it may be too late. If schools are not teaching kids about money and how to manage it, where will they learn those skills? Certain things are better taught at home, money skills being one of them.

After all, in most cases, who better to teach kids these skills than their parents?

There's one small problem with this kind of thinking. Who taught the parents about money and how to manage it? Society assumes that most parents have learned these skills, and then wonders why history repeats itself.

Sabrina and I believe it's time to put a halt to that assumption and start from the grassroots up.

Parents often spend years teaching their kids about the "birds and the bees," but neglect to discuss the subject of money. Some of the most important subjects on personal development, such as financial management and parenting skills, are generally not taught. In fact, parents are often expected to learn by trial and error. Shouldn't there be some kind of handbook, or at least a Quick-Start guide on these subjects?

I remember when Sabrina, our oldest child, was born. Throughout the pregnancy, my wife and I talked with people about things we should do to prepare. We read many books on birthing and went through the Lamaze course. However, we didn't have the slightest idea of how to raise a child. Truth be told, we didn't even do very well with the dog we had at the time. We had to learn everything by doing, through trial and error, and doing the best we could.

* * * * *

Children and adults develop their financial strengths through a combination of the people they are around, the environment they grow up in, and the habits and disciplines they develop as they grow."

Inspirational speaker Jim Rohn, when talking about kids and money in his seminars, often says, "Kids don't lack capacity, only teachers." Another favorite statement of his: "All fortunes begin with a child and a dollar." Therefore, shouldn't kids start learning about money and goal setting while they are still young?

As we begin to teach our children and young adults the skills and discipline to help them reach their full potential, we can also help them organize their dreams and ambitions by creating a list of written goals that they can monitor on a regular basis. We also need to help them set up and maintain a savings plan, so that they can develop the foundation upon which to build their dreams.

In later chapters, we will share with you a series of steps to assist children and young adults with their growth and confidence-building.

Many cultures throughout the world share a respect for money's three distinct purposes: spending, saving, and sharing. It's important for parents to pass these disciplines on to their children by encouraging money exploration and individual creativity. Help your child to develop his or her own personal goals, wishes, and positive experiences. As your children develop strong goal setting and money management habits, they better their chances of reaching their full potential.

Based on Sabrina's and my own adventures, we have generated some suggestions and inspirations that may help you and your child begin to achieve goals by budgeting money for spending, saving, and sharing. Doing so will help you and your children begin to understand how to manage money, and to develop the ideal mindset around money and long-term financial independence.

With the coming of the computer age, it's even more important for kids to understand and know how to properly manage their money when they get it, because now it is so much easier for them to spend their way into trouble.

When I was little, if I wanted to buy something, I had to go to the bank, take my money out, usually with a savings passbook, and go to the store and buy the object. Now, if people want something, they can go to E-Bay or Amazon.com, enter their credit card number, and the item will show up on their doorstep.

As parents, if we don't take a more active role in helping determine the purchasing decisions made by the kids in our lives, then other people will. Consider, for instance, their peers and the media pressure to which they're exposed.

Everyone has the ability to become financially independent, no matter their level of education or current financial status. The only two things needed are discipline and time. Discipline can be learned over time. However, financial independence must be designed. If you wait for it to come by accidentally, you will most likely wake up one day with little time and no money.

The Question of Allowance

One of the most common questions we get asked is if a child should be given an allowance, and if so, how much?

Sabrina and I have found that by giving children an allowance that they are able to use it to buy things they want, they often miss out on achieving the level of satisfaction that comes with earning the money themselves. On the other hand, if you have children do an odd job around the house, say washing the car, or helping you do something that wouldn't normally be considered a chore, pay them the market rate for doing that job. In this way, they will begin to truly appreciate the value of money and the connection between money and what it takes to earn it.

If you do decide you want to give your kids an allowance, one line of thought is to give them one dollar per week for each year of age. For instance, if your child is five years old, you would give the child five dollars a week.

When our kids were little I would tell them that if they needed money for something, they should look around the house and find something that they could do to earn it. They were to bring me a proposal and requested dollar amount, and if it made sense, I would hire them to do the job.

Jennifer, my wife, and I have never given Sabrina or her brother and sister an allowance, but we have often paid them for doing odd jobs. I personally believe this is where the true spirit of entrepreneurism come from. Granted, there are things around the house, like keeping one's room clean, helping with the dishes, or vacuuming the living room that one does a part of the family unit. As an example, I had a goal to write fives thank-you notes a day, so I would have Sabrina put stamps and return addresses on the envelopes, so that they were ready when I got home at night. It was very helpful having those envelopes ready to go. In addition, there were many nights I came home tired, and the last thing I wanted to do was write notes. Those envelopes were there waiting for me, with a sticky note: "OK, Dad, I did my job. Now you can do yours."

Later in the book, we will share different stories of times where making our children responsible for their own money came in handy.

If you own your own business, you can also hire your kids and put them on your payroll. The amount you pay them, however, needs to be equivalent to what you would pay an average employee doing the same type of work.

Make it a goal to become a millionaire, not just for what you will achieve by becoming one, but rather for what it will make of you to become one.
Jim Rohn

CHAPTER 4:
DEVELOPING A MILLIONAIRE'S MINDSET

Mike

Years back, a mentor told me, "You should become a millionaire for what it will make of you to become one. It's the journey from which the greatest benefits will

come."

I took those words to heart, even though at the time, making a million dollars seemed like a large task, if not impossible. At the time, I had three failing businesses, a $100,000 line of credit that was totally maxed out, and $80,000 in short-term credit card debt. In addition, I was the primary caregiver for a six-year-old daughter and three-year-old twins.

One of the businesses was a limousine business with two of our newer limousines in default; the bank had just told me that they were going to come and repossess the limos by the end of the week. Yes, making a million dollars seemed like a great idea, however, at the time, I would have settled with getting my two limousines out of default before the bank showed up with its tow truck.

To make things worse, the three businesses had combined outgoing monthly expenses of $15,000, and monthly revenues of

$8,000. On the home front, $7,500 a month was going out in personal expenses, with $4,500 of stable income coming in to cover those expenses.

I would later jokingly tell people that I was bankrupt and did not know it, so I never filed. My thinking was so far off track, I thought working capital was the available line of credit on my credit cards. Needless to say, the concept of making a million dollars, no matter how exciting it seemed, also seemed close to impossible.

My goal at that time was making $100,000—I didn't even know how I was going to accomplish that. Now my mentor was suggesting that I set a goal to make a million dollars.

When I was a child, my friends and I played the Game of Life. We excitedly tried to get to the millionaire's mansion, rather than land in the poor house. The more we played the game, the easier it became to get to the millionaire's mansion. I wish someone would have told me that real life worked the same way. I would have been as careful of how I reacted to the real-life chance cards as I was when playing the game. I now realized that the better we get at addressing and reacting to life's lessons, the easier it is to get to the millionaire's mansion.

One day, while pondering my situation, I had the opportunity of picking up a very wealthy business man named Mr. Chen at the Seattle Airport, and driving him to Vancouver, where he was going to sign a deal for the purchase of a $200 million office building. On the way to Vancouver, we talked about business.

and I asked him what he felt was one of the greatest lessons he had learned throughout his years and successes.

After thinking for a few moments, he said, "Get used to dealing with the problems or obstacles in business while the zeros are still small. The problems seldom change, just the zeros behind the problems or obstacles change. If you get used to dealing with the problems while they are still small, as your business or financial life grows, you won't get bogged down when challenges arise."

I didn't fully understand what he was saying until a few years later. I made a payroll mistake that cost me $43 and complained about it to my wife over breakfast. Later that day, I was driving the vice president of the MGM Casino to a dinner party. He was on the phone talking to the CFO of the casino, mad and complain- ing to the CFO about the same things I had earlier complained to my wife about. Only his was a $43,000 mistake! In a flash, I understood what Mr. Chen had meant a few years back, and my little $43 dollar mistake didn't seem so bad.

As in the Game of Life, things happen. How we react to the challenges often dictates how things will turn out. When we are playing the Game of Life and we lose, we just pack up the game and put it back on the shelf for another day. In real life, when people lose the money game, they often pack up their dreams, goals, and empty promises, and put them away. However, unlike the Game of Life, there may not be another day.

Income Only Grows to the Level of One's Self-Esteem

I was told by different mentors that my income would only grow to the level of my own self-esteem. While that made sense on the surface, it took some time before the words really started to resonate with me. I became vigilant about what messages I was passing down to my children.

As parents, if we truly want to become wealthy and raise financially savvy children, we need to adopt the proper mindset. I had a strong desire to gain wealth because I knew it would help me do many of the things I wanted to do in life. Yet, it seemed the harder I tried to gain wealth, the faster I would push it away.

On the surface, I wanted to attract and achieve wealth. However, from lessons I learned as a child, I believed deep down that if I acquired wealth, it would make me a bad person and I would lose the respect of those close to me. I had often been told that in order to get wealthy, one had to hurt or cheat other people

On the one hand, I loved business and finances and knew I could make a lot of money in business. However, my subconscious mind would fight me every step of the way. Initially, I thought that I wasn't very lucky or that I didn't know enough. So I kept trying to learn more, hoping that I would find the missing link. The problem was that I was looking outside of myself for the answer, when in fact, the answer had been buried inside of me the whole time.

Sabrina, on the other hand, has a completely different outlook on creating wealth. She grew up learning that money or wealth is available to everyone, when people just stay disciplined and follow the daily habits needed for acquiring wealth. As a young child, she discovered that money is a tool—no more, no less—for helping us bring our goals into realty. For one person, that goal may be to put food on the table. For another, it might be to take a an exciting vacation. For yet another, that goal might be to build a large business or enterprise. No one goal is better or worse than another. Every goal is important to its holder.

You may be wondering why we are discussing self-esteem and belief systems in a book about how to raise financial savvy kids? The answer is quite simple: If you're not careful about your own beliefs about money and wealth, you will pass down those beliefs to your children. The two go hand in hand. If you truly want to acquire wealth, you need to pay close attention to your mindset and the messages you pass on to your children.

Many people share the same fears or concerns about money and finances. Sabrina and I have found that before creating a financial plan, it was first necessary to help parents work through their own beliefs about money and becoming wealthy. Below are some of the more common beliefs with which we've seen clients struggle:

- Most rich people probably did something bad, dishonest, or took advantage of people to acquire their wealth.
- It's more righteous to be poor than to acquire wealth.
- Acquiring wealth takes too much work or struggle.
- I don't feel good or lucky enough to acquire wealth.
- Trying to acquire wealth won't allow much time for anything else in life.
- If I acquire wealth there are certain people in my life who won't like me.
- Having a lot of money means you must be greedy.
- I don't know enough to acquire wealth.
- If I acquire wealth, I might lose it.
- If I really strive for wealth and don't succeed, I'll feel like a failure.
- You can't strive for wealth and be happy at the same time.
- It's not right to make a lot more money than my parents.
- It takes money to make money.
- Striving for wealth can cause stress and health problems.

- Given my past, it would be difficult to acquire wealth.
- I'm too young or old to acquire wealth.
- I don't have the time to manage money; I don't enjoy managing money.
- I don't have enough money to worry about it.
- Financial security comes from having a good job and steady pay check.

Read through this list and see which messages about money you might be carrying around with you.

Building a strong mental foundation about money and wealth is what we refer to as a "millionaire mindset." A large part of becoming financially independent is first developing the proper attitude. Our thoughts can be used to empower us and help us build a huge net worth, or they can run amok, like a drunken monkey, and sabotage our financial efforts. Our financial beliefs come from a combination of our background, the people we associate with, and what we learned about money as children and adults.

These beliefs can be very personal and if not properly managed, can also be very dangerous to our financial wellbeing. Money is mentioned more than any other word in the Bible, including love. That would lead me to believe that money is pretty important, and always has been viewed as such. I personally think that if used wisely, money can become a blessing to many people, but if used unwisely, it can be a time bomb waiting to go off.

In our American culture, we often try to lump people into various groups according to their money and finances, such as the "rich and famous" or the "poor and mistreated." If you look at the media, you see that it often seems to either idolize money and wealth, or look down on it. Great examples are TV shows like Who Wants to be a Millionaire, The Lifestyles of the Rich and Famous, and American Greed.

There are also many common expressions around the pursuit of having money or acquiring wealth, like: "It takes money to make money," "Keeping up with the Jones." There are many ads that promote things to do with money, like: "No interest until June 2020," or "No Credit, No Problem! We love credit chal- lenges."—Sure, at 25 percent interest!

How about another quiz? See if you can fill in the blanks here. "Money is the root of all " or, "It's harder

for a rich man to get into Heaven, than a camel to fit through the eye of a ."

Some people have deep-seated beliefs that to make a lot of money, they have to cheat someone else first, or they are afraid that if they made a lot of money, something bad might happen. I often hear clients say things about acquiring wealth that are fear- based, like: "If I make a lot of money, I might lose it." Or, "What will my friends and family think if I make more money than them?" With thoughts like these, even if they start to make a lot of money, they will find ways to push it away.

Many obstacles stand in our way when it comes to making money, but I think FEAR is one of the largest ones, for it prevents us from taking action. Our mind's primary job is survival, so it will try to protect us even if it's actually hurting us and keeping us stuck inside of our comfort zone. Our financial comfort zone is in direct proportion to our beliefs about money. So when it comes to overcoming fear, it's important to focus on our goals and what we are trying to achieve. Fear can either hold us captive or be a great motivator.

I think Mark Twain coined fear well, when he said. "I have been afraid of many horrible things happening in my life, some of which actually came true." At the end of the day; fear is what we make of it. Zig Ziglar has a great acronym concerning fear, which is: FEAR: False Evidence Appearing Real

It isn't necessary to rid yourself of fear to succeed; it's just important to learn to make fear work for you. One key is learning how to act in spite of fear; this skill can only be mastered through practice. Can you imagine a squirrel saying,

"I'm only going to get a few nuts this year and then take a break, because I can't get enough anyway, so what's the use?" Or, "I'm not going to go look for nuts, because a large animal might eat me." Squirrels grab every nut they can find and bury them away, knowing that winter is always just around the corner.

The first step to moving out of fear and into success is knowing what it is that you want, then making the decision to go out and get it. After that, train your mindset to be able to receive. As you practice these three steps, you will start to see wealth come your way.

On the other hand, if you second-guess yourself or don't believe that you deserve what you want, for whatever reason, you will often push the things you want away from you.

I often observe clients start to build wealth, then mental blocks get in the way and they begin to sabotage themselves or develop the habit of stopping just short of the finish line. They wonder why they don't get all that they deserve.

Remember this adage: the difference between "poor" and "broke" is that broke is a state of your bank account, whereas poor is a state of mind.

There are many people with large bank accounts, yet their mind is set on "poor." I also happen to know a lot of people who have very little money yet carry with them the influence of the rich. If we don't develop the discipline of happiness and success while we are still building our wealth, we probably won't have happiness and the feeling of success later either. When you begin to develop a millionaire mindset, it's important that you continue to re-access your beliefs and make sure that they match up with your goals.

Everyone defines financial independence differently. Some people might need $10 million before they would say they are financially free. For others, that freedom point might be $1 million dollars. One of my favorite definitions for financial independence is: "Financial independence is when your passive income pays for your desired standard of living or lifestyle."

We all have different goals and desires. So we need to continually take a personal inventory of our values and the lifestyle we want to live. Then we can build a financial foundation that will support it.

Some time ago, I learned about a great process for helping a person narrow down his or her passions about money from the book Values-Based Financial Planning by Bill Bacharch. Our values are important, especially with regard to money.

Now, when I sit down with clients, I generally start by asking, "What's important to you about money?" When they answer, I'll follow up with, "What is it about   (whatever they tell me is important to them" that's important to you?" I continue asking, "And what's important about   that's important to you?" until we find their core values or passion. It is at this point we can help them build a financial plan that will capture their inner goals and dreams.

An acronym that I use to remind clients to stay focused on their financial plan is P.E.A.C.E., for financial peace which comes from having control over their finances. Those letters stand for: P as s i on at e — E ner gi z ed — A ppr e ci at i on — C l ea r — Empowered.

PEACE is then broken down like this:

- Make sure you are passionate about what you are doing, and the money will follow.
- Let your passion fill your spirit and keep you energized.
- Remember to show appreciation for all the people who help you along your journey.
- Keep a clear and concise plan for how you are going to reach your financial goals

- Let your passion, energy, appreciative spirit, and a clear and concise financial management system empower you to reach even your highest goals.

Our Subconscious Mind

People tend to follow different mental patterns and repeat common mistakes, such as over-spending, making investments out of emotion and not logic, or putting the brakes on an idea or action that might take them out of their comfort zone.

When a person's conscious mind is busy at work trying to figure something out (a goal, an example), if he or she isn't careful, the subconscious mind may hit the brakes on the person's actions four times harder than the conscious mind would. A person's ability to fully utilize a strong financial management system is also empowered by how well he or she is able to control that subconscious mind.

People are often stuck in their comfort zones. That's because their subconscious minds are trying to get things back to the way they were before they made the changes. The trick with financial management is to trust the system and let it do what it was created to do.

Up to 80 percent of our actions come from our subconscious mind. So that even if we think we are on track, our subconscious mind may have a different agenda, which is why we have to continually be aware of the patterns and habits to which we expose ourselves and our children.

Perhaps an analogy would be helpful. When you use your computer, you may be working on one project and have another project or program working in the background. If the program that's running in the background suddenly developed a virus, it would most likely mess up the project you're currently working on as well.

Our brains operate in much the same way (though much more efficiently). People will install virus protection software on their computers to make sure the above doesn't happen. Yet, they leave their subconscious mind exposed to all the data around them, good or bad. When it comes to creating wealth, our financial beliefs or mindsets will generally come from the following past experiences:

Past Experiences	Present Conditions
1.) Parental influences	1.) Peer groups
2.) Our environment	2.) Financial situation
3.) Religious influences	3.) Physical well-being
4.) School days	4.) Media influences
5.) Teachers, coaches	
6.) Failures	

Changing Our Mindset

To get around subconscious messages, we need to ask ourselves what is the worst and the best we have learned from our past. We then need to bless our past, for the best that has happened, and forget the rest. This is very important to do, so that we don't pass any negative or limiting beliefs around money or finances from our past onto our children. The great thing about the subconscious mind is that it can be reprogrammed through a variety of exercises.

The three most important things for positively changing your subconscious mind are 1) intake (for instance, the books you read and the classes you take), 2) associations (the people you spend your time with), and 3) affirmations or words and phrases that you say to yourself on an ongoing basis. Let's explore these three concepts in a bit more detail.

- **Intake:** Do you like to read, listen to tapes, or attend seminars to expand your horizons, learn about how other people do things to succeed? What kind of messages are you feeding your subconscious?

- **Associations**: Make a list of the ten people you spend most of your time with. Ask yourself: do they build me up or do they tear me down? If a relationship tears you down, ask which of these associations could easily be replaced?
- **Affirmations**: These are the quickest and most effective way to change the words or phrases you use when you talk to yourself. When writing affirmations, they need to be written in the present tense and affirm what is true. Some great affirmations are:

✓ I am a money magnet.
✓ I prosper wherever I turn.
✓ I am healthy and filled with energy.
✓ I achieve the goals that I set.
✓ I grow, push, and stretch.
✓ I easily attract money to me.

Another great exercise is making a list of the things you've done in your life that you're most proud of. The process of writing things down and repeating the affirmations over time will cause them to become your new reality. Beliefs that over time become habits turn into muscle memory. Now make a list of the things you've done in your life that you're most proud of.

- When did you feel you were at your best? That is your muscle memory.
- In what ways have you sabotaged yourself or held yourself back?

Reframing - No matter what happens in someone's life, it doesn't have any meaning except for what that person gives it through his or her own thoughts. The earlier people learn this key fact, the easier it will be to take control of their thoughts and thus what they attract into their lives.

When working with clients, I observe when they have a thought or belief that is standing in their way and holding them back from reaching their financial goals. Then I show them how they can replace those unproductive beliefs with more productive beliefs through the following methods:

Reframing is changing the way a person evaluates the meaning of an action or situation.

Example: I once worked with a client who believed that making a lot of money was wrong because she shouldn't need that much money. After showing her that if she were able to make more money than she needed, she could use the additional money to help a cause that was really important to her. Once she saw the benefit of making more money, how it was larger than her, she started to get excited about making more money. As her beliefs started to change, she started to find ways to attract more money into her life.

Content reframing - which is taking the exact situation and changing what it means.

Example: When my kids were young, I would often be out on a limousine run until two or three in the morning. So we trained our kids to try not to wake me up early in the morning. One morning, after a late-night run, I heard the twins fighting at 7 o'clock in the morning in the kitchen, which was right above our bedroom. Seeing red, I got up and went upstairs into the kitchen. As I entered the kitchen, the twins looked up, saw me, and froze in their tracks.

Sam cried out, "Daddy, we are making you breakfast, and I want to make you pancakes."

Monica cried out, "But Daddy, I want to make you French toast."

Reality set in. Yes, they were fighting, and yes, they had woken me up. But they were fighting over what to make me for breakfast. How could I be mad at them for that?

Looking at them, I said, "Kids, let's play Iron Chef and the secret ingredient is eggs. Let the contest begin!" An hour later, we had two very excited champions, and one very full dad.

Context Reframing - which is drastically changing the way you see, hear, or represent a situation drastically. This means taking an experience that seems to be bad or undesirable and showing how that same behavior or experience is actually an advantage in another context.

Rudolph, the Red-Nosed Reindeer is a great example. While he was teased for standing out with an unusual nose, he was able to turn a potentially dismal situation around.

My personal experience was ending up so far in debt, despite what I knew about money and finance, which made me realize that anyone can make foolish financial decisions, no matter how much they know. So I set out to design a system to help prevent others from going through the pain I did.

Both types of reframing—content reframing and context reframing alter your internal representations by resolving pain or conflict and therefore putting you in a more resourceful state.

Reframing is a wonderful tool when you or your children have false or limiting beliefs. For instance, when our kids tell me they can't do something,

I ask them, "You can't or you chose not to? Either one is fine; just call it what it is." Or if I hear them say, "I could never have or do that; it costs too much," I tell them,

"It's not that it costs too much; it's that you can't currently afford it. So what can you do to earn the money needed to be able to afford it?"

Reprogramming Your Subconscious Mind

Let's look at how to program your subconscious mind with positive self-talk. First you need to reprogram your negative thoughts with positive thoughts. Here are some examples:

- Will I ever learn how to ....? OR I learn everything I put my mind to.
- It's another one of those days! .... OR It's a great day; I'm ready to conquer any challenge put in front of me.

The goal is to replace the negative beliefs with positive affirmations. Again, the affirmations must be in the present tense: "I exercise every day." They must be specific: "I walk two miles every day." They must be personal and honest: "My health gets better and better every day." They must fit your values: "I enjoy being in good health."

If you want your affirmations to quickly take effect, you need to say them daily. You can't change performance by focusing on where you are falling short. You must focus on what you want and act as if you have already accomplished the goal. Your subconscious mind can't tell the difference between reality and fiction.

As Earl Nightingale, author of The Strangest Secret, would say, "What you think about, you bring about." He also was known for saying, "A person will become what he or she thinks about all day long." If people think about being happy or making money, they will achieve it. If they think about their mistakes or reasons they can't do something, they will attract that to them- selves, and life will be very challenging.

Become aware of the language you use around others and your kids. They won't let you down—they will become what they hear you say the most. I always cringe when I hear parents say things like, "You'll never amount to anything" and then wonder why their kids stop trying. Or "You're a slob. You never clean your room," then wonder why their kids grow up and live in a pigsty.

When self-esteem is strong, you have the ability to think logically and move through any challenges. And when your self-esteem is low, you tend to freeze and have trouble moving through your challenges. However, when pride is strong, you tend to rely on yourself, and may close yourself off from opportunities to learn or get support. When your pride is wounded, you might tend to lick your mental wounds and look for outside reinforce- ment. This is when you are the most teachable and open to new ideas. Especially with children, don't lose the teachable moments. Words, when coupled with emotion, lead to powerful results.

Good or bad, our words trigger pictures, pictures trigger emotions, and emotions trigger behavior.

Here are some steps for changing habits and beliefs:

- Awareness – We need to know what to change.
- Understanding – We need to know where the habits or beliefs came from.
- Reconditioning – We need to replace old habits (beliefs) with better new ones.

Our minds are more complex than any machine known to man, yet it's as simple as the computer on your desk. If you put good stuff in, then good stuff will come out. If you put bad information in, it won't run efficiently or effectively. Monitor what you say to yourself and what you hear your children say to themselves. Start putting more good stuff in!

If people are around negativity all the time, and if they're not careful, their self-talk will tend to be negative as well. The importance of self-talk is also talked about in the Bible: "As a man thinketh, so is he." Or, as Jim Rohn said in his Achieving Excellence series, "Don't become a victim of yourself. Forget about the thief in the alley; what about the thief in your mind?" Or "Happiness is not an accident, nor is it something you wish for—happiness is something you design."

Do You Really Know What You Want?

The number one reason people don't get what they want in life is that they don't know what they want, or they spend the majority of their time thinking about what they don't have or what they can't do. Brian Buffini is often quoted at his Turning Point retreats® as saying: "The bigger the why, the easier the how."

Clarity about what you really want in life is essential. It gives you the ability to act. It's not what you don't know; it's what you know that just isn't so, that stops you from succeeding.

Become aware of who you are not, then you can go to work on who you are. Do you continually assess or evaluate your beliefs or habits? If your beliefs are empowering, then you need to keep them. If your beliefs are disempowering, then you need to let go of them. It's very important that you continue to unlearn your old harmful beliefs and replace them with new positive ones.

A few years back, I was very frustrated with someone and was venting my thoughts out loud while cooking dinner. After about three minutes of listening to me complain, Sabrina said, "Dad, would you agree that no one can control your emotions without your consent?"

"Yeah, why?" I said with a puzzled look on my face.

"Well, you know, Dad, you control your thoughts and your feelings, so you can either keep complaining and stay frustrated— or you can chose to think about something happy and allow your inner happiness to come out," Sabrina told me. (In layman's terms, she was telling me to grow up.) And there I was just getting started. I was even starting to feel righteous about being angry at the person, yet the person had no clue he had done anything wrong.

Thanks to my very wise daughter, I hit the rewind button, edited out the angry thoughts, and replaced them with happy, funny thoughts. Then I pushed the play button. I disassociated from what was going on in my mind (my mental chatter), so that I could review it from a distance. It was my choice to hold on to my anger and frustration, or replace them with more pleasant thoughts and words.

You need to reframe the past and program it with the beliefs that will move you toward what you want. In growing your self-esteem, if you choose to neglect one aspect or belief, that will be the one part that will tend to get in the way.

Your beliefs are like blueprints, just like the blueprints provide the design plan for a house. What is your money and success blueprint? Remember, your thoughts lead to feelings, your feelings lead to action, and your actions lead to results. You have many different blueprints. It's up to you to design your desired blueprint for success. What do you want to happen versus what don't you want to happen?

Another great way to develop successful habits is surrounding yourself with people who are doing what you want to become. This is like seeing a house and a neighborhood in which you'd like to live. You can have every investment strategy on the planet, but if you don't have the right mindset, you will probably continue to have money challenges. The true power of having a solid financial management system comes from the following equation:

Thoughts = feelings = actions = results
OR
Action + amplification = results
and results on top of action = confidence

Confidence + momentum = a great attitude and a great attitude brings enthusiasm.

Your income will grow as fast as your self-esteem will allow it. So you need to look at your habits and ask yourself if they will get you to where you want to go. When you handle money properly, it attracts money to you. It's not the amount of money coming in, but what you do with it that counts. In the end, money will only make you more of what you are already.

"Money is only a tool. It will take you wherever you wish, but it will not replace you as the driver. – Ayn Rand"

SECTION TWO:

RAISING FINANCIALLY SAVVY CHILDREN

Set a goal, not only to follow
world-class role models,
but to become a world-class
role model yourself.
—Steve Siebold

CHAPTER 5:
CREATING THE ULTIMATE LEGACY

One's true legacy lies in the greatness of his children!

Again, congratulations! You made it through the hardest part—getting your own financial house in order.

Along my own journey of trying to raise three children, learning about money and business, and how to be a parent at the same time, I learned that the better understanding I had of my own finances, the easier it was to teach sound financial principles to Sabrina, Monica, and Sam. Believe me, there were many nail-biting moments.

Don't feel like you have to master all this stuff before you teach your kids about financial responsibility. We certainly didn't. In fact, it can be a lot of fun to include your kids in the journey. After all, they may become parents themselves one day.

The greatest part of teaching kids about money management is that they have a clean slate to work with. We have found in teaching many different kids these skills, each one brings new insights and excitement. In addition, they tend to learn the concepts at a deeper level, for they have not been as conditioned as we have as adults.

The great part of the money management system presented here is that it is designed to be used by anyone of any age.

While we suggested that you set a goal to create your budget so that you're living on 70 percent of what you make, sharing 10 percent and saving or investing 20 percent, we teach kids to get used to only spending 50 percent of the money they get, save 40 percent and share 10 percent. The goal of this system is for kids to get used to spending only 50 percent of what they make, so that as their income begins to grow, they have already developed the habit of saving a large portion of that income.

In addition, the sooner they learn that when they get a dollar, they can't spend the whole dollar, the better they will be at managing their money.

When Sabrina and I do workshops, one of the first questions we ask the kids is, "Who wants to be a millionaire?" Most will raise their hands. We're still puzzled about the ones who keep their hands down. We then ask them who has to pay rent or a mortgage. Most will giggle. We then ask who has a car payment . Again they will giggle. Finally, we ask them if they have credit cards to pay. Giggles. Our next question is, "Wow! So if we give you each a dollar, you can keep the whole dollar?"

We then pause for a moment, smile, and ask, "Do you all realize that you are already further ahead than many of the adults we work with? You are already on your way to becoming millionaires. All you need now is time, discipline, and a money management system." Their eyes always get really big as they sit there envisioning themselves as millionaires.

We would like to share some fun tools to use when you set out to teach your kids about money. One such tool is the chart below. It demonstrates what would happen if you took a penny and doubled it every day. In our workshops, we like to ask the question, "Which would you choose? A check for $100,000 right now, or a penny now that would double each day for thirty days? Which would you rather have?"

Most participants go for the $100,000 check today. Which would you pick? Now take a look at the chart on the next page.

Did you make the right decision?

Day 1	$ 0.01	Day 16	$ 377.68
Day 2	$ 0.02	Day 17	$ 655.36
Day 3	$ 0.04	Day 18	$ 1,310.72
Day 4	$ 0.08	Day 19	$ 2,621.44
Day 5	$ 0.16	Day 20	$ 5,242.88
Day 6	$ 0.32	Day 21	$ 10,485.76
Day 7	$ 0.64	Day 22	$ 20,971.52
Day 8	$ 1.28	Day 23	$ 41,943.04
Day 9	$ 2.56	Day 24	$ 83,886.08
Day 10	$ 5.12	Day 25	$ 167,772.16
Day 11	$ 10.24	Day 26	$ 335,544.32
Day 12	$ 20.48	Day 27	$ 671,088.64
Day 13	$ 40.96	Day 28	$1,342,177.28
Day 14	$ 81.92	Day 29	$2,684,354.56
Day 15	$ 163.84	Day 30	$5,368,709.12

Need or Want

It's also important to make sure that you teach your kids the difference between a need and a want. Kids often think that everything is a need, even though what they wish for are often wants. Remember, you need food, clothing, and shelter for survival. A want is everything else, a desire.

When your values are clear,
your decisions are easy.
—Brian Buffini

CHAPTER 6 :
MONEY AND VALUES

*Money will only make us more
Of what we already are!*

t's very important to stay true to your values, no matter how difficult it may seem at times. Our kids are always watching what we do, and are often the first to notice when we are out
of sync with our beliefs. Over time, our actions will start to take a serious toll on our children's confidence in us.

Dr. Steven Covey, in his book The Seven Habits of Highly Effective People, talks about something he calls an "emotional bank account." When what we say doesn't match what we do, we make a withdrawal from the mental bank account of others. If we are trying to please others at the expense of our beliefs, we can directly cheat our kids out of a great benefit they would have received if we had stayed true to our core beliefs.

As an example, when my wife Jennifer was pregnant with Sabrina, our first child, we talked about all the different options we had for after she was born. We were both working 60+ hours a week and were now going to have a small baby. I was managing a small real estate company at the time, and Jennifer was the assistant to the president of a successful, medium-sized computer company in the main business district of Bellevue, Washington.

We discussed the possibility of putting Sabrina in daycare during the day. But I didn't like the idea of her being in a daycare all day. Time passed, and we continued to explore different options Finally the day came. My phone rang and it was Jenni- fer's office. The receptionist was almost yelling into the phone.

"Mike, she's in labor, she's in labor. You need to get here right now!" I arrived and Jennifer was talking to someone on the phone, giving an order to someone sitting across from her, and trying to breathe through a contraction at the same time.

We left and drove to the hospital, which was around eight blocks away. We entered the hospital, got checked in, and went straight to the delivery room. Time came to a standstill. The next three hours flew by. Then the doctor entered the room, and thirty minutes later, the sound of a baby crying filled the room. Sabrina was here. Looking down at her for the first time in my life, nothing else mattered but her wellbeing. I got up and went outside, called my boss, and gave him my two-week notice.

I didn't want to put her in daycare all day. Not that there is anything wrong with daycare. In fact, we did decide to utilize their services, but only on a part-time basis. It's just that I had always sworn that Jennifer or I would stay with our kids. And it wasn't fair to ask Jennifer to stay home because she has finally reached the level in her company, she had worked really hard to achieve. If she quit, she would have to start all over.

I had purchased a limousine that I used in the real estate office to take clients to the escrow office. I also knew that the next step in my business plan was to prove that I could build a business from scratch. So I kept the limousine and opened a limousine company. That way, I could take care of Sabrina during the day and learn all I could about the business, and Jennifer would watch her at night while I was on limousine runs.

Two years later, Jennifer gave birth to twins, and I had built the limousine business up to seven cars, opened my own real estate office, and bought a chauffeur school to train great chauffeurs to drive for us.

The plan seemed great, except that because Jennifer was still working 50 hours+ a week and even though she loved what she was doing, her family often called me a bum, telling us that I should have a similar job so she wouldn't have to work as hard. The fact that I was running three businesses, and trying to be the primary caregiver to our three children so they wouldn't have to be in daycare full-time, and Jennifer would have the freedom to grow her career didn't seem to matter much to her family.

What they failed to realize was that even if we put our children in daycare full-time so that I could also hold down a full-time job, Jennifer would still work the same schedule. She loved her job, and if she wanted to advance in the company, those long hours were what the job demanded.

How many fathers do you know who work 60 to 70 hours a week throughout their career? When men work those long hours, it's looked upon as being OK, simply because they are men. In fact, they are often looked at with a great deal of respect. Yet, if a woman wants to build a career, and works the same number of hours, she is often looked at as being either a negligent mother or a supermom.

Unfortunately, as a man, I have been accused of being a negligent husband, but never a superdad. There were many days I would wonder if I was crazy for trading in a six-figure income to build what often felt like a failing business, along with being the primary caregiver for our three children. However, I knew if I stayed focused on my dream business and tried to be a great example for our children, we would be able to make great things happen. Looking back, I'm so thankful for the relationship that I have been able to build with our children, and the limousine business was a great classroom.

One of my goals with this book and our workshops is to help make it easier for other dads who want to be stay-at-home fathers or serve as the primary caregiver for their families.

As parents, we need to provide for our children and our family. However; if one parent has the ability to provide for the family and loves what they are doing, it shouldn't matter what gender they are. Those roles can also change over time. That is why it's so important to have a comprehensive financial plan in place when starting your family.

When Jennifer and I first got married, I remember telling my mom that I was going to try to get a good job, so Jennifer could be a stay-at-home mom. My mom snapped back, "Do you have any idea how much it costs to raise kids these days? You will both have to work if you want to be able to put food on the table. Stay-at-home moms went the way of the dinosaur a long time ago."

"Just you wait. I will get a good job, and she will stay home," I snapped back.

"Good luck with that," she said, walking off in a huff.

That shows how little I knew about my wife at the time. She is a great mother. However, it would have driven her crazy to be at home with the kids all day. She loves the hustle and bustle of working and being able to help her clients.

As parents, it's important to continually try to stay congruent with our values and beliefs about money and finances, and to discuss these values with our children. Life has a way of giving us "teachable moments" as a way to help teach values to our children. When such moments arise, it's very important to use them as life lessons. One such moment came when the twins were six and Sabrina was nine.

We were driving home from church and the kids were telling us what they learned in Sunday school. They related that it's wrong for parents to hit or abuse their kids, and how we need to make sure we never do that. I couldn't help wondering at the time why they seemed so intent on making sure Jennifer and I under- stood how wrong it is for parents to hit their kids. We had certainly never hit them or given them the feeling that we might.

Jennifer and I remained silent as they lectured us on the merits of child rearing, and the evils of child abuse, even though they were only nine and six at the time. We arrived home and everyone went about his or her day. Then Sabrina asked to talk to me.

"Dad, Dad, I need to talk to you, but you have to promise that you won't get angry." Not the words a father wants to hear from his daughter.

"Daddy, do you promise if I tell you something, you won't get angry?"

"I don't know. It depends on what it is," I answered.

"No, Daddy, first you have to promise you won't get angry and spank Sam."

Thinking that her reasoning was coming from what they learned in Sunday school today, I asked Sabrina, "Sabrina, have you seen me spank Sam before?"

"No, Daddy, but you have to promise you won't spank Sam or yell at him too bad, or I won't tell you. Okay, Daddy?"

"All right, Sabrina, I promise," I said.

"Okay, Daddy, you see, I saw Sam playing with a sock full of quarters on his bed, and when I asked him where he got them, he said, "Oh, Mommy and Daddy have a big jar of quarters under their bed, and I took some so I could buy candy at school. They don't use them anyway."

"He what?" I could feel the anger starting to grow. "Now, Daddy, remember. You promised."

"I remember, Sabrina, but you don't understand. He stole money from us."

"I know, Daddy, that's why I told you, but he doesn't understand what he did."

"Still, Sabrina, stealing is wrong, and he has to learn that it's not ok to steal."

"I know, Daddy, that is why I told you, but you promised you wouldn't punish him too bad."

I couldn't believe I was having this conversation with a nine-year-old.

"SAM, GET IN HERE NOW!" I yelled.

"Daddy, you promised!"

"Yes, Daddy?" Sam said as he ran into the room. He then looked down and saw the sock of quarters on the bed. His face suddenly changed from a smile to shock as he looked at the sock, the look on my face, then over at Sabrina.

"Sam, go to the bathroom and wait for me there!"

"Sabrina, I know that you are concerned about your brother, and even though it may not feel like it at the moment, what you did by bringing this matter to my attention was a very grown-up thing to do. Sam is lucky to have a sister who loves him enough to look out for him like you did. I am very proud of you!"

"Daddy, you promised!"

"I know. I'm going to go and talk to him," I answered as calmly as I could.

As I entered the bathroom, I could tell that Sam knew he was in trouble, yet he didn't seem to really know why.

"Sam, did you put the quarters in the sock?" "Yes," he said in a little voice.

"Sam, did you take the quarters from the jar that is in our room?"

"Yes."

"Sam, did we say you could have them?" "No, but you don't use them for anything."

I could feel my anger starting to grow. How could he steal from us? Where had we gone wrong as parents? How had our sweet little boy turned into a thief?

A memory flashed through my mind. When I was about Sam's age, I had taken $5 out of my mom's purse, and went down to the corner store to buy gum. The store owner called my mom and asked if she knew what I was doing. My mom told him to send me home, and as soon as I walked into the house, my stepfather grabbed me by the arm and took me to the bathroom.

As if it were yesterday, I recall him putting me over his knee and being spanked once for every dollar I had taken. What made it worse was that he was a chef so his hands were like iron. He then told me that if I ever stole money from my parents again, I would be spanked twice as hard and twice as many times. Leaving the bathroom in tears, I swore I would never steal from them again— and I never did.

Here I was, 35 years later, in the same position except that this time, it was my own son. I remembered how much it hurt to get spanked, but it taught me to never steal from them again. (I did shoplift a few times after that, until I got caught and brought home by the police, but that's another story for another time. So did the paddling really teach me the lesson of not stealing?

Looking down at my little boy, all I knew was that he was not going to become a bank robber if I had anything to do about it. He was my son, I was his father, and it was my job to make sure that he grew up with proper values. He had to be taught a lesson.

Yes, I promised Sabrina that I wouldn't spank Sam. I also knew that I wasn't going to raise a thief. Being spanked by my stepfather hurt, it hurt a lot, but after all, I turned out all right.

So I sat down on the toilet seat, grabbed Sam by the arm and put him over my knee. Not knowing what was happing, Sam started to cry.

"Daddy! Daddy"!

Again, looking down at him, I couldn't help thinking about the conversation we had earlier that day on the way home from church, and how Sabrina made me promise her that I wouldn't spank Sam, even though I had never spanked him before.

Then it hit me. I was about to discipline Sam the same way I had been disciplined as a child, without first questioning why. Sure, the spanking deterred me from stealing from my parents, but was physical punishment the right answer?

First of all, I had promised Sabrina that I would not spank Sam. If I did, I would violate her trust. Secondly, Sam didn't really understand why he was about to be spanked. Sam had spent the morning learning that it's not good for parents to hit their kids, so what would my spanking him tell him? That stealing is bad, and that if you steal, you will be spanked, or worse. Even though I would be doing what I was taught by my own parents, a spanking would or could seriously undermine the trust of both my children.

I believe that in life, things often happen for a reason, I call those "life's lessons." The series of events that led up to this moment was one of these.

Looking down at Sam, I moved him off of my knee and stood him on the floor in front of me.

"Sam, you know that I love you very much, right?" "I know, Daddy."

"Sam, do you also know that it was wrong to take the money from your mother and me?"

"I didn't think you used the quarters for anything."

"They were in our room, plus you knew that they didn't belong to you, right"?

"I guess."

"When you go into our room and take something from us, it's the same as stealing. And that is wrong, so I need to punish you. I'm not going to spank you. However, it's very important that you

know it's wrong to take something that doesn't belong to you, even if you don't think it's being used. I want you to go and get your Yu-gi-oh cards and bring them here."

Sam went into his room and brought a medium-sized, black and white box full of Yu-Gi-Oh cards he has been collecting for about a year. People gave him the cards as presents, or he saved up money and purchased them himself when he got the chance. He had a pretty good collection going.

"Sam, please hand me the box full of cards." I then got up and went outside with the box to where my car was parked, which was next to a garbage can and the garage. I opened the car door, then the garbage can lid, threw the box of cards toward the garbage, and then went back inside. As I entered the house, I saw Sam standing in the middle of the room, crying.

"Daddy, why did you throw my Yu-Gi-Oh cards away?" "Why did you take quarters from me and use them to buy candy at school?"

"My cards! Those are my cards!"

"And those were my quarters in your sock!" I replied.

Crying harder now, Sam said, "But it took me so long to collect them. Those are my cards!"

"Sam, come outside with me."

He followed me outside and we walked over to the car. I open the car door and asked Sam to look inside.

"What do you see?"

"My Yu-Gi-Oh cards! But I saw you throw them away."

"It only looked like I threw them away, Sam. Do you know why I didn't throw them away?"

"No," he answered.

"Sam, I didn't throw them away, because they belong to you. Sure, your mother and I gave you some of them, but other people have given them to you for your birthday or for Christmas. Plus, you saved up and bought some of them with your own money. You see, Sam, if I had thrown them away, it would be the same as if I stole them from you. How did you feel when you thought I threw them away?"

"Mad and sad. They are my cards," he answered meekly. "You're right, Sam. They are your cards. They don't belong

to me. Well, Sam, that is how I felt, when you took the quarters from me. Can you understand now, why it's so bad to take something that doesn't belong to you? Stealing or taking something that belongs to someone else will cause them to feel mad, or sad, like you felt."

"I'm sorry, Daddy. I didn't mean for you to be sad," giving me a hug.

"Sam, how many quarters do you think you took from us?" "I don't know."

I went to my room and got the jar of quarters, which I dumped on the table and stacked some up. "Sam, how big was the pile of quarters that you took?"

Sam looked down at my pile. "I think I took maybe this many."

We both looked at the pile of quarters. Again, I asked Sam, pointing at the pile of quarters, "So you think you took about this many?"

"Yes, I took about that many."

"Sam, let's count and see how much money this is. Okay?" "Okay, Daddy."

We counted the pile of quarters and it came to nine dollars and fifty cents. "Okay, Sam, you need to pay your mother and me back for the quarters that you took from us. Do you understand why?"

"Yes."

I picked up the box with Sam's Yu-Gi-Oh collection and told him that I was going to use them for collateral toward his loan.

"Daddy, what is collateral? And what is a loan?"

"A loan is when you borrow something like money from someone with the promise to pay the person back. And collateral is something that has value, that you give the person who loaned you something, like money, to keep just in case you don't pay them back." I was in teaching mode.

"An example would be this house. When we bought it, we didn't have enough money to buy it, so we went to a bank, and borrowed the money to buy the house. Now the house is collateral for the loan. If we don't pay the bank back the money they loaned us to buy this house, they can take the house and sell it to get their money back." He nodded.

"Sam, I trust you and know that you will pay your mother and me back for the quarters you took from us. However, I am going to keep your Yu-Gi-Oh collection as collateral. When you pay us back the $9.50, you can have your Yu-Gi-Oh cards back, okay?"

I then wrote up an IOU that said, "I, Sam Raber, hereby promise to pay my mom and dad back the $9.50 I took from them." I then had him sign and date the IOU.

"Daddy, how am I going to get the $9.50 to pay you so I can get my cards back?"

"Well, Sam, I need to take someone to the airport and while I'm gone, I want you to look around and think of some things that you can do to help me around here and how much you think your time is worth."

When I returned home, Sam had put together a list of about ten things that Sam could do to earn some money. The next day, Sam and I agreed on a value for each task, and he went to work on completing them. Within three weeks, Sam finished the last task and had raised $11. He gave me $9.50, and put the remaining $1.50 in his save jar.

I returned Sam's Yu-Gi-Oh collection and we took the IOU outside and burned it. Sam experienced his first mortgage burning ceremony. That was the last time he ever took anything that didn't belong to him.

Keep your eyes open for such teachable moments with your kids.

If nothing ever changed, there would be no butterflies.
—Anonymous

CHAPTER 7:
CHANGE IS INEVITABLE

Teaching Children to Embrace Change

If you believe a big change is on its way, always make sure that your foundation is firmly in place and that you're ready for it. I'm a firm believer that the more prepared you are, the fewer chances there are that something will go wrong. Proper preparation is always the best defense. It always amazes me how people ignore the signs until it's too late. Then, when something goes wrong, they scramble to catch up.

In our household, Jennifer and I always have told our kids that change is the only constant in life. Therefore, we and they always need to be pre-planning for what they want to have happen. A great book for both adults and children to discuss change is Who Moved My Cheese, by Spencer Johnson.

The better kids are used to dealing with change, the easier it will be for them to adjust to changes as they grow older. Granted, with very young children, consistency is important to establishing a sense of stability and developing a strong foundation. However, as they grow older and changes occur, use such moments for teaching and openly discuss the pros and cons of change.

Probably one of the biggest strengths I developed early on was my ability to adapt to change, because it felt like my life was changing constantly.

One big change for our whole family was making the decision to move to Milwaukee from Seattle to provide our kids with the opportunity to be closer to their grandparents I believed the move would be a key factor to moving my dream business forward. Jennifer, however, felt like she was starting all over, for even though she often complained about her job in Seattle, she had still loved it.

We decided we would give it 30 days, and if it was truly the right time to move, then everything would fall into place. We put our house on the market at what I believed was on the high side of the market. I began talking to another limousine company about buying my company.

Within three days, we had a full-price offer on our house that would also allow us to stay in the house until the kids were done with school for the year. A week later, our offer on a house in Milwaukee was accepted. Negotiations with the other limo company were well underway.

Jennifer negotiated with her Seattle boss to let her keep her job and work from Wisconsin, since much of what she did was Internet-based anyway. For Jennifer, that meant it was business as usual, just from a different location.

On July 5, 2005, we pulled up in front of our new house in Milwaukee.

Something told me she also needed to have a back-up plan, so I created the shell of a business. Three years ago, on November 16 at 4:15 p.m., I walked into our front door. Sabrina greeted me with, "Dad, Mom just got fired. I think you'd better go see if she's all right."

When I walked into Jennifer's office, she was just staring at her desk in shock. "My boss just called. He said he was taking the business in another direction and that I would not be part of that.

He then told me he had just disconnected all network connections to my computer, so I need not bother finishing out the day."

My first response was that he hadn't thought this through, and that he needed Jennifer much more than she needed him. I asked her what she would like to do now.

"I don't know, Mike. I really like what I'm doing. I like selling computers and working with colleges on their hardware and software needs. And I really like my clients. We have built up great friendships over the years."

I then suggested that she call all her customers, tell them that she had been let go, and also to tell them how much she had enjoyed working with them.

An hour or so later, Jennifer emerged from her office, a broad smile on her face. She told me many of the customers had not liked the company she had worked for, and that if she were to work for another similar company, they would follow her.

"But I don't know anyone here. How will I get a job with another computer company?" she asked, somewhat dismayed.

"Maybe it's time to open your own company then," I replied. "It's not that easy," she objected.

"Just for the fun of it, if you were to open a company, what would you call it?"

After thinking a while, Jennifer said, "I don't know. I kind of like JR Microsystems."

I went back downstairs, turned on my own computer, and completed the online paperwork to set up Jennifer's LLC. I then told her that on Monday, she should call all her customers and tell them she was now working for JR Microsystems, LLC. She is the newly appointed president, and will need their help in growing the company by sending her referrals.

She followed my recommendations and on Monday learned how many of her customers believed in her and her new business. Her business has grown 30 percent every year since then without making many changes to her day-to-day activities.

Because we had followed the savings plan set forth in this book, and had an emergency fund set up, we could cover our living expenses for a year, if need be, without having to tap into our savings or investment accounts. Between what I was making and some savings, we were able to cover our family's expenses. Thus, Jennifer was able to grow her business over the course of the next year without having to take any money out of it.

Change will certainly happen, but if you plan for it, everything will work out in the end. Change is not bad; it's how we react or respond to change that matters.

"The world as we have created it is a of our thinking. It connot be changed without changing our thinking." – Albert Einstein

CHAPTER 8:
TURNING DREAMS INTO REALITY

Teach your children to shoot for the stars

Consistent goal-setting is the cornerstone to achieving all great dreams. Teaching our children how to set goals and having them develop the habit while they are still young
will help lay the path to many great accomplishments.
Children do this instinctually when they come to us and say "Mom, Dad, when I grow up, I want to be a fireman." They might say they want to be an astronaut, a teacher, or even a superhero. Usually, they come up with meaningful occupations. Unfortunately, as they grow, they tend to shy away from such dreams.
One of my major pet peeves is hearing parent say, "Oh Tommy, stop living in make-believe. It's time for you to grow up." Phrases like that are the killers of all great intentions and imaginings. Make-believe is the place where all great accomplish- ments are born. As parents, it is essential that we encourage our children to shoot for the stars, to set goals for their dreams, and go to work on making them a reality.
It's equally important to help them navigate the world of reality. There's certainly nothing wrong with children having a goal that seems very large or way off in the future. If they are passionate about the goal, at some point in their lives, with some help and support, the goal could be accomplished.
When teaching kids to set goals, it's important to establish a deadline or benchmark, even if it's way off in the future.
A goal is far more effective when it is written down, for what gets written down, gets done

.A goal also needs to be measurable. Kids (and adults) need to be able to measure their progress. Especially if they have a large goal, it helps to take the large goal and break it up into smaller mini-goals

I remember Sabrina coming home from a doctor's appointment when she was about two. She said to Jennifer and me, "Mommy, Daddy, when I grow up, I'm going to be a doctor."
We both looked at her and said, "That's great, Sabrina. You'll make a wonderful doctor." Later that week, I bought Sabrina a small doctor's kit from Toys-R-Us as a reminder of her new goal. Amazingly, her stuffed animals all got physicals from her the next day. Before long, there wasn't a sick stuffed animal anywhere to be found. Years have passed, yet her dream to become a doctor remains, even though it has taken on different life forms.

When Sabrina was about eight, at dinner one night, she looked at Jennifer and said, "Mommy I decided that I am going to open a clinic near your office. That way, if you get sick, you can come to my clinic during your lunch hour."

Smiling, Jennifer said, "That's wonderful, Sabrina, that will be so convenient. And I'll get a discount, too, because I'm your mother, right?"

"Well, I guess I could give you a 10 percent discount." Sabrina said, looking somewhat annoyed.

"What? Only a 10 percent discount?" But I'm your mother."
"Yeah, Mom, but I have to pay everyone who works there,

the person who checks you in, or the nurse who takes your blood pressure,. That's a lot of people."

"Hey, even a 10 discount is better than what we are getting now, Jennifer. Besides, you'll be able to go there on your lunch hour." I said, laughing.

We knew then that the dream of becoming a doctor was still burning strong. A year or so later, Sabrina and I were at a networking event, and I overheard her asking Monty, one of my clients who was a residential home builder, if he would consider helping her build a building, when she grew up, near where her mother worked."

Surprised, Monty asked her, "What is the building for?"

"Oh, I want to open a clinic near my mom's office, and when I heard you and my dad talking about the house you just built, I was thinking that if I can't find a building that fits my needs, then I could just build one." Sabrina replied.

"Well, Sabrina, I normally only build houses, but for you, I'll make an exception." Monty said, looking at me and smiling.

"Thanks, Monty, I look forward to doing business with you in the future," Sabrina replied, a big smile plastered across her face.

I'm not sure what surprised me more, that fact that we were having this conversation or that it seemed so natural.

That's what's so great about how kids think. They don't get caught up with all the details; they see a picture of what they want and the rest is expected to come naturally.

As far as Sabrina was concerned, the deal was as good as done, and didn't need any further thought until she was ready to open the clinic.

I, on the other hand, was thinking to myself, first Sabrina needs to finish medical school, which she needs to pay for first. Then she needs to create a business plan for her clinic, and make sure there is a viable market for her clinic. After all, Jennifer doesn't get sick very often. Then, after searching for a suitable location to lease, if there wasn't any available, she would have to acquire a suitable lot, do all the engineering work on the lot, and finally, one to two million dollars later, be ready to build a building.

Boy, I was already tired just thinking about it! And what are the chances of Sabrina still wanting to be a doctor when she grows up?

What's so great about kids is that they don't let fear or doubt get in their way. They set a goal and go for it.

Whether old or young, if we can see it as if it's already completed, we can bring our dreams into reality. It may take time, a lot of work, or even the help of many other people. However, if the desire is strong enough, it can be done.

I often tell our kids that they can't always control the results, but they can control their actions. The right actions will, in time, yield the results they want.

Sabrina played the flute for the Milwaukee Youth Symphony Orchestra and set herself a goal of becoming a member of a group called the Philharmonic Orchestra, which is extremely hard to get into. She had to try out, and then wait for about a month before she knew if she got in. The day the results arrived, Sabrina was having lunch with a friend of hers who was already in the Philharmonic Orchestra.

Two letters came to the house and knowing how important it was to my daughter, I brought them to her. Sabrina opened the first letter and saw that she had gotten into a group called Cham- ber Flutes. Sabrina then opened the second letter and sat there with tears running down her cheeks.

"Why, Dad, why? I wanted to get in the Philharmonic Orchestra so bad."

"I know, Sabrina."

"I got wait-listed. Why? I practiced so much!"

"I don't know Sabrina. What I do know is that in life we get three answers: Yes, no, or not now." It's not yes, because you didn't get in yet. It's not no, because you're wait-listed. So that just means that it's not now. Maybe you will have to wait until next year or, maybe later this year. Remember, you can't always control the results, but you can control your actions.

"Do me a favor, Sabrina," I said, hugging her. "You have Chamber Flutes from 4:30 to 6:00 on Mondays, and the Philhar-monic Orchestra practices from 6:30 to 9:00 on Mondays. Right?"

"Yes, Dad, that's right."

"Since you're going to be there anyway, go to the Philharmonic Orchestra, help set up, talk with your friends, and envision how you would feel and what you would be doing if you were in the orchestra, okay?"

"Okay, Dad."

The first week of practice came, and Sabrina helped set up. Her friends came in and she talked and joked around with them, and she stood where she would stand if she had gotten into the orchestra. She visualized how she would feel if she were part of the orchestra. Then it was time for it to start, so we had to leave.

Sabrina walked out, looking down at the ground with a sad look on her face. The second week came and we repeated the process, and again, when it was time for the orchestra to start, Sabrina left with a sad look on her face. The third week came and we repeated the process, and again it was time for the orchestra to start and Sabrina left with a sad look on her face.

I was starting to second-guess myself. I couldn't help thinking that I might unintentionally be setting Sabrina for continued disappointment. I hated to see her leave looking so down in the dumps. I asked Sabrina if she liked to help set up and hang out with her friends.

She answered, "Yes, but I really wish I could stay and play with the orchestra."

I told her to be patient and her turn would come.

The following week, Sabrina was at a swim meet. While I was waiting for her, I got a call from the senior conductor for the Philharmonic Orchestra, who said, "Mike, I opened up another seat for Sabrina, and I would really like her to play with us." Then he asked if she would still like to be part of the orchestra?"

I said, "Yes, she has been praying every day for this opportunity. I will let her know and we will see you on Monday."

"Great, I look forward to seeing Sabrina next week," he said.

Not only did she finish out the year in the Philharmonic Orchestra, she won a contest and was able to compose a piece for the Chamber Flutes.

In 2012, she got in the highest-level orchestra at the Milwaukee Youth Symphony Orchestra, called Senior Symphony. This past summer, they toured Vienna and Prague and represented the United States in an international music contest, where they placed second in the world.

We can't always control our results. However, we can control our activities. When we do the right activities, (granted it may take time, patience and the help of other people), in time we will receive our desired results.

Once visualized, goals are very powerful motivators. The only challenge that both adults and children run into when they have a really large goal, is that it can become overwhelming. It's hard to determine what to do first. The first step to avoid over- whelm is to see the goal as if it is already completed. The next step is to back engineer the steps to the beginning.

As an example, Monica, Sam and Sabrina's sister, has wanted a puppy for about two years now. About once a month, she would ask Jennifer and me if we could get a puppy.

Jennifer always answered, "No, Monica, we already have three fish. A puppy is too much work."

A few months ago, Monica found a really cute puppy and brought a picture to show us. "Mom, Dad, look at this puppy. It's so cute, and it only costs $750. Can I get it? Please, please can I get it? I'll pay for it."

Now, when your 14-year-old daughter says "only $750" when talking about a dog (puppy or not), that should be the first reason to worry.

Jennifer looked at Monica, and said, "$750, huh? And you will pay for it?"

"Yes, only $750. I'll pay for it and we can pick it up in four weeks."

Okay, tell you what," Jennifer replied. "You have three weeks to come up with the money, and you can't take any money out of your bank account. You have to raise the money from scratch."

"Really, then I can have my puppy?" "That's correct," Jennifer said.

"Okay, Mom, let me fill this out and then please sign it." Monica grabbed a pen and wrote out the following.

I, Jennifer Raber, will let Monica Raber buy her puppy if she can raise the money within three weeks.

Jennifer signed the sheet and gave it back to Monica. I think that Jennifer secretly hoped Monica would say, "Raise $750 in three weeks from scratch? That's impossible. Okay, then, I guess I can't have the puppy."

Jennifer must have forgotten that since our children were small, we have instilled in them the belief that if there is something they want, and it's a sound purchase, and they have the ability to raise the money to buy it, if they set a goal to get the thing that they want, we would support their decision and help them figure out a way to raise the money.

Monica started to back-engineer her goal: $750 in three weeks. That would be $250 a week or $35.71 a day. If she could sell a bank Sabrina sold called a Moonjar® for a profit of $5, she would have to sell a total of 150 Moonjars®, or 50 Moonjars® a week, or 7.14 Moonjars® a day.

Later that day, Monica called the breeder and negotiated him down to six hundred and fifty dollars. She then asked me if she could go to different networking meetings with me so she could sell the Moonjars®. I said "Yes", and she was able to raise the money in just short of three weeks. Monica is now the proud owner of a black Cockapoo puppy. Who, just happens to be sleeping on the floor here next to me as I write this. Thank you, Monica, for persevering and bringing your goal into reality. Since, Lucy is the cutest puppy.

The trick to teaching children how to set goals, when they are young, is starting with small goals, encouraging them that they can reach the goal and helping them through the process, until the goal is reached, at which point, you want to praise them, and help them celebrate the fact that they reached the goal, no matter how large or small the goal may appear.

To a young child, even acquiring something for a dollar is a big deal. Always remember, the true growth lies in the journey, not just in reaching the goal. Many times they may even change their mind or change the goal before they reach it.

I remember when Sam was about ten. We were at a store near our house, and he saw this really cool Lego set of an air- plane. He asked if he could get it, so I told him it looked fun and that he should set a goal to get it. He then started saving his money up, so he could buy it. About a month later, he had saved enough money in his spend jar to buy the Lego set, so we went to the store to buy it. When we got there, Sam noticed that they no longer had the one he wanted, but they had one he liked even more. The only problem was that is cost $20 more.

I told him we could go to another store and see if they had the one he saved for. But Sam said he would rather have the new one. I asked Sam how long he thought it would take him to save for the new one, and he said, "Probably one more month." "Wow, Sam, one more month," I said. "What if they sell out of this one, too?"

"I don't know," he replied. "If they do, then we could go to another store and find it."

"Yea," I said, "that's a possibility, tell you what Sam; I will put $10 toward your new goal. That way you only have to save another $10. How does that sound?" We went home, I gave Sam some jobs I needed help with and within two days, we were able to go back to the store and buy the Lego set.

When we got home, Sam went up to his room to put the Lego set together. I went up to check on him an hour or so later, and he was sitting there looking at his Lego set with a sad look on his face. I asked Sam what was wrong and he answered, "Dad, when I finished putting the Lego set together, I started to think about how it only took me an hour to put the set together, yet it took me five weeks to save up the money." I reminded him that even though it only took him an hour to put the Lego airplane together, it would always be there for him to look at, and he could still play with the Lego pieces.

"I know" Sam said. "I just couldn't help thinking that it took so long to save up the money and maybe there was something better I should have saved for."

Surprised that Sam was having such thoughts, especially since he was only ten, I smiled and said, "Sam, that's a very important lesson you just learned. When we set a goal to buy something, or when we see something we want to buy, we have to ask ourselves, is the thing we want to buy really worth the money we will have to spend?"

He looked interested, so I went on. "So what determines whether it's worth it or not? The time spent earning the money compared to the time spent using the thing you buy? Or the joy the thing you just bought gives you? Let's say, Sam, that instead of buying the Lego set, you spent five weeks saving up the money and then used the money to go to a fancy restaurant. Would the food or the two hours you spent dining in the restaurant be worth the five weeks it took to save the money?"

"No way. There's no restaurant that cool," Sam replied. "What if it only took you two hours to save the money, then

would it be worth it"? I asked.

"Yea, if it only took two hours," he answered.

"So the benefit achieved needs to be equal to or greater than the cost, correct?" I asked.

"I guess so."

"Do you feel then that the benefit you received from the Lego's wasn't equal to the cost?"

"That's right. After putting it together, I'm not sure if it was worth it or not."

"Well, Sam, sometimes when we decide we want something, even though it seems so great at the time, in the long run, the value really isn't there. The trick is to learn from that activity and try to make a better purchasing decision the next time."

"Sam, what if it had only taken you two hours to earn the money to buy the Lego set? Would it have been worth it then?"

"Yea, but it didn't," Sam said.

"True. So in the future, you have two choices: be more careful about the things you save up for, or make more money so you don't have to save as long, or preferably do both. However, Sam, for now, celebrate the fact that you set a goal to buy the Lego set, and you were able to make it happen in only five weeks. I think that's pretty cool. Sometimes in life, we have to remember to enjoy the things we have. And you have to admit, that is a pretty awesome Lego airplane you just built."

"Yeah, I guess you're right," he answered, a grin on his face once again.

* * * * *

Charitable Thoughts and Stewardship

When teaching our children to set goals, it's important to also have them set goals around sharing/tithing, or things that will allow them to help other people. This helps show them that they have the ability to make a difference in the world, no matter how big or small the contribution. In essence, by doing so, we are teaching them the importance of becoming good stewards One of my favorite quotes around saving and sharing is a phrase coined by John Wesley: "People should earn all they can, save all they can, so they can give all they can." If kids develop the habit of giving back while they only have a little bit of money, they will keep that habit when they have a lot.

Here's a great example. A friend of mine started his money management system because he was spending more than he made. Over the years, he was able to build his fortune to the point that he is living on only 10% of what he makes and using the rest to help other people.

In addition, I have found that when you set a goal for the benefit of someone else, that goal takes on an energy of its own. When setting charitable giving goals, it's good to find organizations or causes that you and/or your children believe in, and set goals around helping those groups. It's also good to share your goals with other people, no matter how far off they may sound.

Sabrina became involved with the YMCA when she was in pre-school and had a lot of fun there. When she was around eight, she joined the YMCA basketball team and played with the Blue Jays. While playing basketball at the Y, she heard her coaches talking about a campaign to raise money for kids who couldn't afford to attend the YMCA but wanted to. She thought it sounded like a great program, so she wanted to get involved.

Sabrina and I started to attend the meetings and we set a goal to raise money for the campaign by selling her Moonjars®. We also started to teach workshops at the YMCA for the kids who were attending the YMCA after school. At one of the meetings, Sabrina learned about a special group of about twenty business people, called the Chairman's Roundtable. She asked how someone could become a member of the Chairman's Roundtable, and was told that members have to own a business and contribute $1,000 to the campaign.

Later, on the way home, Sabrina told me that she wanted to become a member of the Chairman's Roundtable and set a goal of raising $1,000 to fulfill the criteria. The challenge was that she was a kid and she only had four weeks to raise the money.

At the next meeting, one of Sabrina's coaches asked her if she would give a small speech about how she was trying to raise money. She agreed and walked up to the front of the room, which was filled with 100 adults. Sabrina introduced herself as Sabrina Raber with Children and Beyond, gave her speech and concluded by looking at the people sitting around the Chairman's Roundtable.

Her final words were that she was happy to be part of such a great cause and looked forward to becoming a member of the

Chairman's Roundtable." The whole room broke out into ap-
plause, and one of the members of the Roundtable said they would
be honored to have such a great young lady as a member.

I'm pretty sure he thought she was referring to when she was
older. Little did anyone know that four weeks later, Sabrina would
become the youngest member of the Chairman's Roundtable in the
history of that YMCA.

Two weeks after Sabrina's presentation, the Roundtable held a
black-tie event at an exclusive mansion on the shore of Lake
Washington. It was intended as a donor appreciation gala to thank
members for their contributions to the campaign and to discuss the
following year's fundraising campaign. Sabrina received her
personal invitation on fancy letterhead. She could bring one
guest; lucky for me, she chose to take her dad. She also needed a
new dress and a ride to and from the dinner, so it all worked out
well. When our goals are clear, there's no telling what we can do.

Goal-Setting as a Family

Another great tool for teaching our children how to set and
achieve goals is to set family goals.

When Sabrina was nine, and Monica and Sam were six, we
wanted to attend a three-day conference called Mastermind, an
annual event put on by Brian Buffini. One year, it was scheduled
to take place at Disney World in Florida. As a family, we decided
our goal was to attend the Mastermind event. This meant we would
need to save the money to pay for the trip well before going to
Florida. We figured it would cost around $3,000 for the family…
so that's the amount we set as our savings goal.

Every Sunday, we would review our budget and see how much
we had achieved toward our goal.

One day, I got home and asked my family, "How does take-
out pizza sound for tonight?"

Sabrina looked up and said, "Yeah, pizza sounds great, but is
pizza in the budget?"

Stunned, I answered, "No, pizza isn't in the budget, but I'm tired and don't feel like making dinner tonight. Pizza sounds good, doesn't it?"

"Mastermind, Dad. Remember Mastermind? We'll all help you make dinner tonight." All three kids chimed in.

I hadn't even considered Mastermind, but for the kids, the goal of going to Florida and Disney World was much stronger than pizza.

Several months later, all five of us went to Disney World and the Mastermind event. The trip was paid for before we got on the plane, and Sabrina, Monica, and Sam each had $50 to spend when we got there. Never once did they ask if Jennifer or I could pay for something they wanted. They were really careful not to buy souvenirs until the last day, so that they could spend their $50 wisely on what they really wanted.

There is no greater feeling as a parent than knowing that you have given your children the self-reliance to make wise financial decisions when needed—whether that decision involves purchasing a 50-cent piece of candy, a souvenir from a trip, or a new car. It's important to teach our children the difference between needs and wants early on. The earlier they learn to manage their money, the easier it will be for them to acquire wealth, which begins with setting goals and "reverse-engineering" the necessary steps to achieve those goals.

The Power of the Written Goal

When establishing goals, nothing is more powerful than putting those goals into writing. I believe the reason that New Year's Resolutions tend to fail is that they're not written down. In my experience, once things are put into writing, they tend to be accomplished. To really add momentum to your goal, include a picture or photo next to the words to help you visualize your goal or goals more strongly.

Here are only some of the reasons to put your goals into writing. Written goals:

- Create a sense of purpose and anticipation
- Are great confidence builders
- Help strengthen focus and reduce wasting time
- Reduce subconscious conflicts or objections
- Provide guidelines for good decisions
- Help you work through mistakes and obstacles you might encounter
- Strengthen your resolve to accomplish the goals

Putting your goals in writing helps to bring forward your abilities and competencies to accomplish the goals.

When setting your goals, it's important to have a deadline or date by which you want the goal accomplished. Also, imagine or visualize what it will feel like to accomplish that goal. Be aware of "why" you want to accomplish that goal, for that will help you overcome self-imposed or outside objections.

There are any number of ways to write down your goals. One is to make a list of your goals. Another is to write your goals as if you have already achieved them. For instance, if you are trying to lose weight, you could write: "It's January 31. I weigh 190 pounds, am full of energy, and in excellent shape," rather than stating "I want to lose 25 pounds by January 31."

You can also create a Dream Board or Vision Board. Cut out or take pictures of your goals or things you want to acquire, then paste them onto a large piece of paper to make a collage or visual portrayal of all the things you would like to bring into your life. The one on the next page is one that Sabrina created some years ago.

You can also help younger children set goals with "Dream Bubbles." Visit our website, www.childrenandbeyond.com and go to the Resources tab to print out a copy that you can fill out with your children, or create your own.

My Dream Board

Become vice president of the student council

Get all A's for the end of the quarter **A+**

Get in to a good college

Make the basket ball team

Make the varsity on the swim team

Go to Seattle

Go to Europe

Sabrina's
Dream Board

Dream Bubbles

Fill in the bubbles with your wish-upon-a-star dreams

Dream Bubbles for
younger

We began this book by sharing Sabrina's dream of bringing financial literacy to both children and their parents. We discussed Sabrina's and my ongoing journeys to bring our dreams into reality. as well as the many challenges.

We talked about goal setting, both for children and adults, and how important it is to write those goals down. For the financial system presented here to work, it also requires patience, discipline, and commitment.

In addition, Part of the journey involved the strive towards financial stability and financial independence. It meant creating a wealthy mindset, designing a living budget, net worth statement, developing and following a plan for paying off debts, and growing wealth while implementing a strong and practical financial management system.

We hope that through the stories we have shared with you throughout the book, you will discover that no matter how large or small your dream, no matter how young a child, any dream, through faith, patience, perseverance, and the help of others, can be fulfilled. Now let's explore the system to further help you get there.

Congruency between your vision and your action will determine whether you are a visionary or a dreamer.
—Steve Siebold

SECTION THREE:

THE SYSTEM - SIMPLE STEPS TO BECOMING A FINANCIALLY SAVVY PARENT

CHAPTER 9:
TAKING THE CHAOS OUT OF
MONEY MANAGEMENT

Creating a Living Budget

When you set out to build a strong financial foundation, the first and most important part of that foundation is implementing a solid and consistent money management system. The two most important tools used for maintaining a money management system are a living budget and a net worth statement. Once you have a living budget and a net worth statement in place, it's important to start looking at your goals and how much money you need to reach those goals.

I've found that when most people hear the words "financial planning" or "money management," they associate those with accounting or bookkeeping. Or they might find themselves saying something like, "Sure, financial planning is important if you have a lot of money, but I don't have very much money, so what's the difference?" Or, "I don't need to worry about a budget, or a financial plan yet. I don't have that many expenses, and I always have enough money to cover my expenses." Or, "Sure money management is important, but I don't have the time now to worry about it."

On the surface, these might sound okay. However, your success depends on the degree of your planning. You've probably heard the saying, "If you fail to plan, then you are planning to fail,"

Or, according to Jim Rohn, "The difference between the rich and the poor is that the rich invest their money and spend what's left, and the poor spend their money and invest what left." True financial planning is not only taking action—it is a mindset as well.

All of nature understands that to survive you must put food away for times when it's hard or when you really need it. Squirrels spend all summer collecting nuts and burying them for win- ter. Bears hibernate in the winter, so that they don't burn too much body fat, because once everything freezes, it's hard to find food. Yet, as consumers, many people live for today and forget about planning for tomorrow.

I often tell clients that if they continue to manage their money the same way as they did for the past couple of years, then their finances will look the same next year as they do now. If that is okay with them, then great, However, if they want more, they need to change what they are doing today. Said another way, are they on track or off track to reaching their financial goals and making their dreams come true?

Many people don't like budgets because they think of budgets as limiting. However, a budget is only a scoreboard that shows you where your financial outflow compares to your financial in-flow at any given point in time. Most people wouldn't drive in a strange city without a map or first getting directions, yet they often run their most valuable assets or resources without a financial road map.

Years back, Brian Buffini taught Sabrina and me to call a budget a living budget, a term we really like, because it's impor-tant to create a budget that flexes around your lifestyle. Your budget or spending plan is the vehicle to get you from point A to point B financially, and money is the gas that fuels the vehicle. How much you make isn't as important as how much you save and spend. It's very important to always watch for spillage in your spending. When you don't know how much or how little you really have, there is no way of knowing how much you can actually afford to spend.

Your budget acts as a general guideline, but it's important that you assess where your spending is within your budget at least once a month. Then make adjustments as necessary. As an example, let's say you spend on average $400 a month on food. That is where you set your budget. You then have guests from out of town who stay with you for two weeks. You may end up spending $500 that month on food. So that month, you need to make an adjustment for food in your budget. Otherwise, it might feel like you just blew your budget, when in fact, you just needed to account for an increase in food costs because of your company.

We have found that many people don't set reasonable expectations when creating their budget, so they keep blowing it month after month and eventually give up. When implementing a money management system, it has to give you a greater sense of control, otherwise it becomes restrictive and frustrating, not freeing.

When you begin the process of creating a money manage- ment system, the first tool you need to put in place is a living budget. Your budget should be made up of two parts: incoming money or income, and outgoing money or expenses. Income If you are self-employed or are paid by commission based on your sales or production, establishing your income can be an even bigger challenge, because you may not always know how much you will be getting or when income will be coming in. If you are self-employed or tend to have inconsistent income, we would recommend that you also have a business budget. However, it's more critical that you have a personal budget. We will go into more detail of the difference between the two later. For now, it's more important to discuss the process for separating your business income from your personal income. Once that is done, you need to create a living budget for your personal expenses.

A living budget is built around a consistent inflow and outflow of revenue and expenses, so, if you have irregular income, it's even more important that you have a system in place to track your income and expenses. The system we think works the best is to set up a separate account that you treat like a business account and put all your irregular income into it. You then take an amount that you can consistently pay out and pay yourself once or twice a month just as if it were part of your salary. It should look something like this

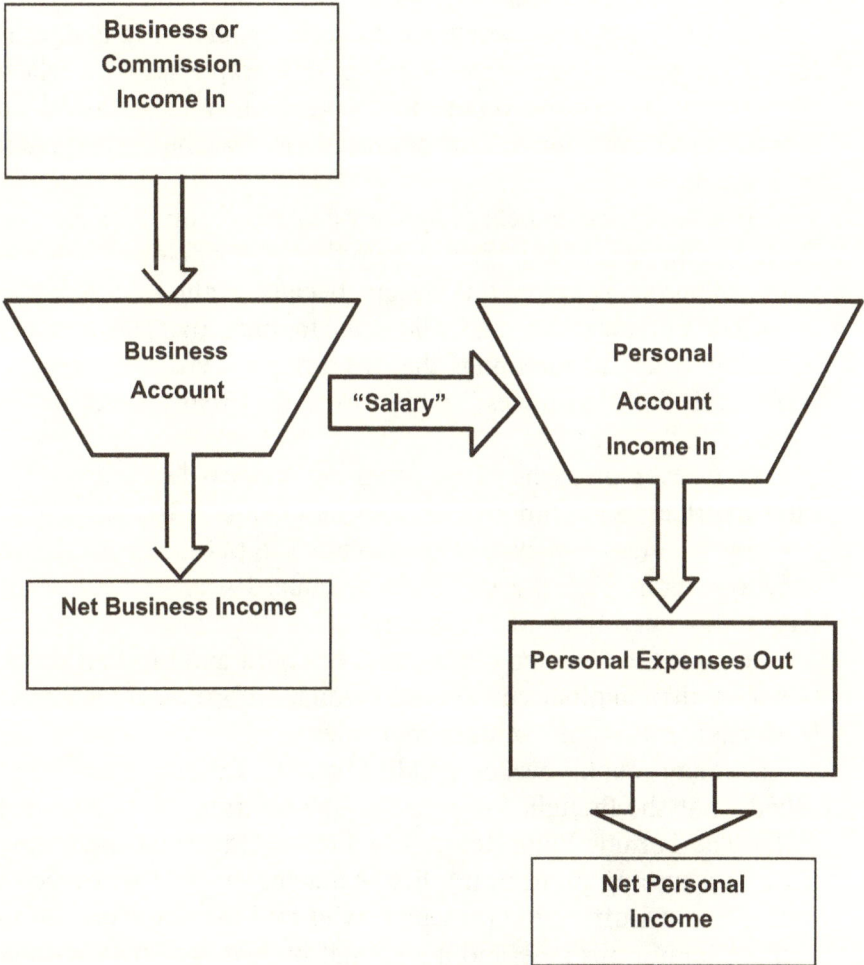

```
┌─────────────────┐
│ Business or      │
│ Commission       │
│ Income In        │
└─────────────────┘
        │
        ▼
  Business          "Salary" →  Personal
  Account                       Account
                                Income In
        │                          │
        ▼                          ▼
┌─────────────────┐        ┌──────────────────┐
│ Net Business     │        │ Personal Expenses │
│ Income           │        │ Out               │
└─────────────────┘        └──────────────────┘
                                   │
                                   ▼
                           ┌──────────────┐
                           │ Net Personal  │
                           │ Income        │
                           └──────────────┘
```

The starting point for creating your living budget for self-employed or commission-based people.

Over the years of helping clients create their living budgets, we have found that no two budgets look the same. The reason for creating a living budget is to serve as an account of your ongoing revenue and expenses. However; it is also the foundation upon which to build your goals and dreams. Many great plans are smothered by unnecessary expenses.

The first step we recommend to create your living budget is listing all your expenses on the Monthly Expenses Worksheet (Worksheet 101) shown on the next page. You can also download a spreadsheet from our website or create your own on the computer or in a notebook.

Then rank these expenses by their degree of importance.
Brian Buffini taught us a great system that he refers to as "ABCing your expenses." We liked this system, because it allows us to better prioritize our expenses and allow us to plug the leaks in our spending. Many of the things that we thought were "must haves" were really "like to haves," things we didn't really need, or we weren't ready for.

As an example, when I was running Newcastle Limousine, I built the fleet to six limousines and one town car. If you remember, my business expenses were around $15,000 a month. I was only averaging $7,500 a month in revenue. I was so busy in the day-to-day operations of the business that I had never stopped to create a budget. I maxed out the line of credit and my first check bounced, then another and another, which unfortunately were the lease payments on one of our limousines.

That day was my wake-up call. I went to a friend of mine and asked what she thought I should do. She referred me to an event called The Turning Point Retreat®. I attended the event and it truly became a turning point in my life. After the event, I was able to talk to Brian Buffini, the presenter, who told me that I needed to prepare both a business and a personal budget, and then cut out anything that wouldn't adversely affect my business if I went a week without it.

**Expense
WorkSheet 101**

	Write down your monthly expenses then total them up at the bottom Name	Total Amount	Type F / V / I / 0	√
1				
2				
3				
4				
5				
6				
7				
8				
9				
10				
11				
12				
13				
14				
15				
16				
17				
18				
19				
20				
21				
22				
23				
24				
25				
26				
27				
28				
29				

After running the numbers, I only really needed two limou- sines and one town car given the number of limousines runs I was doing. The remaining vehicles were costing more to keep in our fleet each month than they were bringing in. So I sold four of the limousines and opened a corporate account with a rental car company. That way, I could rent a town car, van, or SUV when I needed one.

That one change cut $6,000 a month in expenses out of my budget. I then made the commitment to build my business one hundred percent by referral, and canceled our Yellow Page advertisements, which cost $5,000 a month. I was now once again operating in the black.

Back to creating your own living budget, or spending plan, for those of you who think the word "budget" is a four-letter word. On the next couple of pages, we will walk you through the process of creating a living budget from start to finish. We created all the worksheets with the formulas to add every- thing up for you, and placed them on our website,

ww.parentingthatmakescents.com for you to download at your convenience. There are several blank rows in case you have an expense that isn't on the expense worksheet. Just add it in the expense column. We would suggest that you fill out the work sheets first on the website, then print them out for your records.

For the sake of the following exercise, we are only going to use six months' worth of expenses. Ideally, you will want to go back twelve months. We have already added up each expense and placed them in the proper monthly expense slot. The first step to creating a living budget is to make a list of the things you spend money on, such as your mortgage or rent, food, insurance, utilities, entertainment, and so on. On the following pages, you will find examples of both a blank and a filled-in expense log. Go to our website, www. Parentingthatmakescents.com and enter all of your expenses.

With the following illustrations, we pre-filled the worksheet as if you had a monthly revenue of $7,500. You're living on 90 percent of your income, sharing 3 percent of your income (charitable donations), applying 3.5 percent to short-term savings and 3.5 percent to long-term savings or debt reduction.

We will discuss those percentages in a later chapter. Because savings and sharing follow your income, those are treated as variable ex- penses rather than fixed expenses, like rent or mortgage pay- ments. We know this process can seem daunting at first, but we hope these worksheets will provide you with good guidelines.

Now back to the process. Once you have listed all your expenses, go through your checkbook, credit card statements, and bank statements. Add up all your expenses for the month in each category and write them on the monthly expense log. Once you have all your expenses listed on your monthly expense log, add up the different months and put the amount in the total column on the monthly expense log. If you use the worksheets on the website, the columns will add up for you automatically.

MONTHLY EXPENSE LOG

	Jan	Feb	March	April	May	June	Total
Salary							
Other income							
TOTAL INCOME							
EXPENSES							
Household sup.							
Toiletries							
Food							
Mortgage							
Electricty / Gas							
Water & Sewer							
Phone / Internet							
Clothes							
Education							
Other Insurance							
Health Insurance							
Home Maint							
Donation							
Gas							
Auto Rapair							
Pharmacy							
Medical / Dental							
Presents / toys							
Travel							
Entertainment							
Property Tax							
Fed / State Tax							
Short term savings							
Long term savings							
Intrest / Bank fee							
TOTAL EXP.							
Net Income							

	Jan	Feb	March	April	May	June	Total
Salary	7,500.00	7,500.00	7,500.00	7,500.00	7,500.00	7,500.00	45,000.00
TOTAL INCOME	7,500.00	7,500.00	7,500.00	7,500.00	7,500.00	7,500.00	45,000.00
EXPENSES							
Household sup.		16.59				16.33	32.92
Toiletries	103.87	298.12	87.22	39.44	92.92	45	666.57
Food	336.22	816.93	482.79	458.87	606.82	502.67	3204.3
Mortgage	1594.64	1594.64	1594.64	1594.64	1594.64	1594.64	9567.84
Electricty / Gas	298.01	181.34	166.97	106.84	101.35	109.07	963.58
Water & Sewer			141.77			141.77	283.54
Phone / Internet	74.87	75.34	79.35	70.34	76.57	79.87	456.34
Clothes	18.96	92.69	301.57	258.87	518.93		1191.02
Education	79.5		364.58	375.23	28.64	76.71	924.66
Other Insurance	70.5		579.84	70.5		579.84	1300.68
Health Insurance	512.79	512.79	512.79	512.79	512.79	512.79	3076.74
Home Maintenance	11.61	175		31.38	66.72		284.71
Furniture		2100					2100
Donation	225	225	225	225	225	225	1350
Gas	281.37	262.35	304.23	337.39	294.3	284.49	1764.13
Auto Auto'	782.2					749.22	1531.42
Pharmacy	43.58	23.22	28.45	34	29.54	36.4	195.19
Medical / Dental	128			21.51			149.51
Presents / toys	50	22.69	30		171.06	50	323.75
Travel	53.31					408.53	461.84
Entertainment	89.35	110	70.79	123.78	89.78	129.28	612.98
Property Tax	3072.21		1576.19			1576.19	6224.59
Fed / State Tax				1060.8			1060.8
Short term savings (3.5%)	262.5	262.5	262.5	262.5	262.5	262.5	1575
Long term savings (3.5%)	262.5	262.5	262.5	262.5	262.5	262.5	1575
Intres Interest / Bank		50		25			75
TOTAL EXP.	8350.99	7081.7	7071.18	5871.38	4934.06	7642.8	40952.11
NET INCOME	-850.99	418.30	428.82	1,628.62	2,565.94	-142.80	4,047.89

Depending on the type of mortgage that you have, your property tax and homeowner's insurance may be escrowed or added to your monthly mortgage payment. If that is the case, then you wouldn't have to put money aside for your property tax and homeowner's insurance. If you have the choice of paying the property tax and insurance yourself, we would recommend doing this to see what each costs and so that you have more control.

When lenders escrow property taxes and insurance, they always hold a couple months of extra payments aside. Depending on the amount of your property tax, that could mean a few thousand dollars. Over the course of the year, the interest you could earn on that extra amount can add up. Plus, if you should change lenders, that is easier to do if you're in control of your payments. If you do pay taxes and insurance yourself, however, set aside the monthly allocation of your property tax payment so that you have it when it's time for you to make the payment.

When you fill out your worksheet, you will see that some months you may have a negative balance. In our example, in January, the first property tax payment required half-down, then the rest could be paid over the next four months. There was also a large auto repair bill. To stay on track, it's also important to have an emergency fund in place, along with budgeting for things like your property tax.

We would recommend that you use the monthly expense log going forward to track all your expenses for the month. Once you have your monthly expenses written in the Monthly Expense Log, you can begin formulating your budget. When you do this, we recommend going back at least six months, and ideally a full year, so you can get a more accurate running average. If it's too much work to go back a full year, then go back as far as you can.

Here's an example of how to find out how much you're spending using your electric bill. Month one, your bill is $298.00, month two it's $181.34, month three it's $166.97, month four, it's $106.84, month five it's $101.35, and month six it's $109.07. Total up the six months: $298.01 + $181.34 + $166.97 + $106.84

+ $101.35 + $109.07 = $963.58. You should have $963.58 in your TOTAL column.

Just like you did with your electric expenses, follow the same process for all your other expenses. Once you have all your expenses written down on the Monthly Expense Log, you can begin formulating your living budget.

The next step is to take each expense out of the total expense column on the monthly expense log and carry it over to the Expense Worksheet 101, shown on the next page. (Also available on our website to download or fill in).

You have different kinds of expenses each month. Once you have all your expense totals carried over to the expense work-sheet, go through your expenses and decide if they are fixed, variable, irregular, or other expenses. In the Type column, add an F for Fixed Expense, a V for Variable Expense, an I for Irregular Expense, and an O for Other Expense.

• Fixed Expense: Expenses you have to pay every month that stay the same. Example: your mortgage or rent, car loan, health insurance, childcare, your savings plan, etc.

• Variable Expense: Expenses you have to pay every month, but the amount changes month to month. Example: Utilities, food, gas, entertainment, etc.

• Irregular Expense: Expenses you have to pay quarterly, twice a year, or even annually. Example: different types of insurance or property taxes. Depending on your city, you may have to pay them monthly, or every two months over the first six months of the year, or even twice a year. Even though they are a monthly liability, we recommend that you treat them as an irregular expense.

• Other Expense: Expenses that tend to be a one-time expense, or expenses that are not very frequent. Example: a family trip you take once a year, clothes, a new dining or bedroom set, a large repair, etc.

Expense WorkSheet 101

	Write down your monthly expenses then total them up at the bottom Name	Total Amount	Type F / V / I / 0	√
1	Household Expense	32.92	V	
2	Toiletries	667.57	V	
3	Food	3,204.30	V	
4	Mortgage	9,567.84	F	
5	Electicty & Gas	963.58	V	
6	Water & Sewer	283.54	I	
7	Phone & Internet	456.34	V	
8	Home Maintenance	284.71	V	
9	Clothes	1,191.02	O	
10	Education	924.66	V	
11	P & C Insirance	1,300.68	I	
12	Health Insurance	3,076.74	F	
13	Furntiure	2,100.00	O	
14	Donation	1,278.00	V	
15	Gas	1,764.13	V	
16	Auto Repair	1,531.42	O	
17	Pharmacy	195.19	V	
18	Medical & Dental	149.51	V	
19	Presents & Toys	323.75	O	
20	Travel	461.84	O	
21	Entertainment	612.98	V	
22	Property Tax	6,224.59	I	
23	Federal & State Tax	1,060.80	O	
24	Short Term Savings	1,491.00	V	
25	Long Term Savings	1,491.00	V	
26	Interest & Bank Fees	75.00	V	
	Monthly Expenses	40,713.11		

Once you have all your expenses labeled as fixed, variable, irregular or other, carry it over to the appropriate worksheets. Start by taking your fixed expenses and entering them on Worksheet 102: Fixed Expenses, shown below.

WORKSHEET 102: FIXED EXPENSE

Write down your monthly expenses then total them up at the bottom Name	Total Amount	Divide by # of months	Monthly Expense	
1 Mortgage	9,567.84	6	1,594.64	
2 Health Insurance	3,076.74	6	512.79	
Total Expenses	12,644.68	6	2,107.43	

Once you have all your fixed expenses carried over to Worksheet 102, add up the monthly expenses, then divide by the number of months of expenses to find an average monthly expense, in this case, 6 months.

Next, take all your variable expenses, those marked with a "V," and enter them on the Worksheet 103: Variable Expenses. Once you have all your variable expenses carried over to Worksheet 103, add up the monthly expenses, then divide by the number of months of expenses to find an average monthly expense.

Lets say the total cost for electricy like whats on Worksheet 103 on the next page for six months is $963.58. Divide that total by 6, or 963.58/6, equals $160.59 a month. Your monthly average electric bill will be $160.59, which is what you then enter in the monthly expense column. If you have twelve months' worth of expenses, do the same thing but divide by 12.

Some expenses, like your electricity bill, will fluctuate throughout the year. It will be lower in the summer when the weather is warm and higher in the winter when the weather is colder. So, if you only track your electricity expenses during the winter, your average will be skewed. That is why the longer time period you have, the more accurate your average monthly expenses will be.

WORKSHEET 103: VARIABLE EXPENSES

Write down your monthly expenses than total them up at the bottom Name	Total Amount	Divide by # of months	Monthly Expense	
1 Household Expense	32.92	6	5.49	
2 Toiletries	667.57	6	111.26	
3 Food	3,204.30	6	534.05	
4 Electicty / gas	963.58	6	160.60	
5 Phone / Internet	456.34	6	76.06	
6 Home Maintenance	284.71	6	47.45	
7 Education	924.66	6	154.11	
8 Donation	1,278.00	6	213.00	
9 Gas	1,764.13	6	294.02	
10 Pharmacy	195.19	6	32.53	
11 Medical / Dental	149.51	6	24.92	
13 Entertainment	612.98	6	102.16	
14 Short term Savings	1,491.00	6	248.50	
15 Long term savings	1,491.00	6	248.50	
16 Interest / Bank fees	75.00	6	12.50	
Total monthly Expenses	13,590.89	6	2,265.15	

Now that you have carried over your fixed and variable expenses, look at Worksheet 101 and take all your irregular expenses, marked with an "I," and enter them on Worksheet 104: Irregular Expenses, by when you have to pay them (quarterly, every six months, or annually). Divide each irregular expense by the number of months to get the average monthly expense, which you'll then enter in the Monthly Expense Column.

WORKSHEET 104: IRREGULAR EXPENSES

Write down your monthly expenses then total them up at the bottom Name	Total Amount	Divide by # of months	Monthly Expense	
Every Two Months				
1 Property Tax	6,224.59	6	1,037.43	
Quarterly				
1 Water & Sewer	283.54	6	47.26	
2 Other Insurance	1,300.68	6	216.78	
Total Expenses	**7,808.81**	**6**	**1,301.47**	

As we mentioned earlier, there are things like a vacation that you take once a year; or furniture that you buy only every couple of years. You labeled these with an "O." Throughout the year, expenses will come up that don't fit anywhere else. Take these expenses and enter them on Worksheet 105: Other Expenses. Take each of your other expenses divide them by the amount of months of expenses that you have, and carry that average over to your monthly expense column.

WORKSHEET 105: OTHER EXPENSE

Write down your monthly expenses than total them up at the bottom. Name	Total Amount	Divide by # of months	Monthly Expense	
1 Clothes	1,191.02	6	198.50	
2 Furniture	2,100.00	6	350.00	
3 Travel	461.84	6	76.97	
4 Presents / Toys	323.75	6	53.96	
5 Auto repair	1,531.42	6	255.24	
Fedural & State Tax	1,060.80	6	176.80	
Total Expenses	**6,668.83**	**6**	**1,111.47**	

Once you have the monthly running average for each expense, carry all monthly expenses over to the appropriate place on the Living Budget Worksheet, shown on the next page. If there is something that you want to do or buy that is outside of your normal budget, find out how much it will cost, divide the amount by twelve, and plug it into your budget. After your budget is completed, enter your monthly income. Now add up all the different columns, and then subtract your total income from your total expenses. The difference is your net monthly income or loss.

Congratulations! You have created your living budget. Are you ahead or behind?

After you have your living budget completed, and you've determined if your monthly cash flow is either positive or negative, you have a great place to start to build a stable financial future. You will begin to have a firm grip on your spending and income potential. It is at this point that you will be able to really start to become financially free. This is actually a very simple process. All it takes to become financial independent is discipline, consistency, and time.

- The discipline to create a spending plan and stick to it, no matter how hard it might be.
- The consistency to follow your plan each and every day.
- The time to let your investments grow and start to yield your desired results

So that you can see the complete system at a glance, we have it laid out over the next few pages.

A, B, C Your Expenses
Now that you have gotten your living budget down on paper, we recommend that now you "A, B, C" your expenses. This will help you prioritize your expenses. When sitting down with clients and helping them A, B and C their expenses, we are often able to help

them free up as much as $200 or $300 a month, which can then be used to pay down debt, or save and invest for the future. Break down all your expenses into the following:

- A expenses are needs like housing, transportation, food, clothes, etc. These are fixed or variable expenses that you have in order to cover your basic needs.
- B expenses are needs that you can do something about now. These expenses are for things that you need or even want, but you have control over when you get them. B expenses are like a new suit or dress, cable TV, or a new car when the one you have still runs fine.
- C expenses are wants or things that you would like to have if you had the money. These are on your wish list.

Step-by-Step Summary

- Step 1: Create a Monthly Expense Log
- Step 2: Fill out Worksheet 101 then categorize as Fixed, Variable, Irregular, and Other expenses (F, V, I, O)
- Step 3: Fill out Worksheet 102: Fixed Expenses
- Step 3: Fill out Worksheet 103: Variable Expenses
- Step 4: Fill out Worksheet 104: Irregular Expenses
- Step 6: Fill out Worksheet 105: Other Expenses
- Step 7: Complete Your Living Budget

With this example, there is a net income of $714.50 (the last number on the right at the bottom). You could put that money in your checking account for later or apply it to your emergency fund, if you are in the process of building one. Use this to pay down debt or save/invest for the future. We recommend that you do a combination of all these actions, which we will explain in the next section.

YOUR LIVING BUDGET

Income	Amount	Transportation	Amount
Wages	7,500.00	Gas / Fuel	294.02
Business Income		Insurance	216.78
Interest / Dividends		Repairs	255.24
Total Income	7,500.00	Transportation Totals	766.04
Expenses		Entertainment	
Home		Eating Out / DVD Rentals	102.16
Mortgage / Rent	1,594.64	Movies / Plays	
Utilities	207.86	Concerts / Clubs	
Internet Connection	76.06	Entertainment Totals	102.16
Home / Cellular Telephone			
Home Repairs / Maintenance	47.45	Health	
Furniture	350.00	Health Club Dues	
Property Tax	1,037.43	Health Insurance	512.79
Home Totals	3,313.44	Life / Disability Insurance	
		Medical / Dental	24.92
Daily Living		Prescrip / over the counter	32.53
Groceries	534.05	Health Totals	570.24
Child Care / Education	154.11		
Dry Cleaning / Grooming		Vacations	
House cleaning / supplies	116.75	Plane fare	76.97
Daily Living Totals	804.91	Accoummodations	
		Food	
Financial		Rental Car	
Loan Payments		Vacations Totals	76.97
Credit Card Payments	12.50		
Short term Savings	248.50	Dues / Subscriptions	
Long term Savings	248.50	Magazines / Newspapers	
Federal / State Tax	176.80	Dues / Sub Total	
Financial Totals	686.30		
		Total Income	7,500.00
Personal		Total Expense	6,785.52
Clothing	198.50	Net Income / Loss	714.50
Gifts	53.96		
Charitable Donations	213.00		
Personal Education			
Personal Totals	465.46		

For the purpose of this illustration, you are living on 90 percent of your income, sharing 3 percent of your income (charitable donations), applying 3.5 percent to short-term savings and 3.5 percent to long-term savings or debt reduction. We will discuss these percentages in a future chapter. Because sharing and savings follow your income, those are treated as variable expenses rather than fixed expenses.

What if your expenses are more than your income? If your expenses are more than your income, you have three choices: increase your income, reduce your expenses, or do both. Many people use credit cards, lines of credit, and so on to cover the difference, and then wonder why they end up in financial trouble. Whenever you use a debt instrument to balance your budget, it's like being in a hole and trying to dig yourself out from the bottom. The only way to get yourself out of the hole is to stop digging. It's the same way with your finances: until you cut the spillage in your spending, and have more money flowing into your budget than you have flowing out, you will always be playing catch up.

Once your income exceeds your expenses, you have a surplus that can be plugged into your savings plan. It is at this point that you can really start to get ahead financially. The most important thing now is to stay true to your plan, and let the system do its job. All the income you have coming in should be treated equally unless you are self-employed. In that case, you need to use a portion of your net business income to cover your personal salary. However, if you get a bonus, don't treat it like normal income and spend it. Apply it straight into your cash flow system. If you do want to buy something with part of it, make sure that you have a predetermined percent for how much you want to save out of the bonus. Otherwise, you are liable to spend the whole bonus.

It will take about a year to get a good feel for your budget once you begin living according to your spending plan or living budget. If things at times feel out of control, don't worry—that's normal. The most important part of keeping a living budget is monitoring it on a regular basis. Your life will change, and you will have unexpected expenses throughout the year. So you will need to adjust your budget to meet those changes. Remember, if you don't know how much money is going out, you can't plan for the money that comes in.

The goal of this money management system is to help you create a financial plan that will empower you to take control of your finances. All great financial plans start with a systemized living budget.

The system is structured so that all you need to do is move from one page to another. Print the worksheets off our website, www.childrenandbeyond.com and fill them out by hand, or fill them in on the website itself.

Congratulations! You have now completed your living budget, and A, B, C-ed your expenses. The next chapter will walk you through the process of creating a net worth statement.

Many of life's failures are
people who did not
realize how close they
were to success
when they gave up.
—Thomas Edison

CHAPTER 10:
DETERMINING YOUR NET WORTH

It's a lot easier to create a net worth/equity statement than a living budget, so you've got a major step behind you. When putting together your net worth/equity statement, you're
looking at your assets compared to your liabilities, at one point in time. Many banks require a net worth statement when you apply for a loan or line of credit.

•   Asset – Something that has value, like a house, car, jewelry, a business, different investments, or collectables.

•   Liabilities – Something on which you owe money or have borrowed against, like a mortgage, car loan, or credit cards. There are short-term and long-term liabilities:

•   Short-term debt or liability: Something you will generally pay off within a year, like a charge you put on your credit card.

•   Long-term debt or liability: A long-term liability is a loan that will take more than a year to pay off, such as a car loan a car or a mortgage.

As you did with the living budget, print out the worksheets on our website, and fill them in as you go along. We will walk you through the process step by step, using examples on the following pages. In case you want to fill the worksheets out as you go through this excerise, we included the blank worksheets are our website, www.childrenandbeyond.com

- Step 1: List all your assets on Worksheet 106: Personal Assets. Once you have all your assets listed, add up their values and put the total on the bottom of the worksheet. Carry that total to the Net Worth/Equity St atement.

- Step 2: List all your liabilities on Worksheet 107: Personal Liabilities. Determine if they are short-term or long-term liabilities. Add up their values and carry the total over to the Net Worth/Equity Statement.

Once you have your assets and liabilities listed, do you have a positive net worth or a negative net worth? This is the score card from which you can start to build wealth. All good financial plans should incorporate a process for paying off one's debt. In the next section, we will walk you through a step by step process for paying off your debt. You will start by paying off your short-term debt, then begin applying the payments towards your long-term debt until you're debt free. Once you are debt free, you are able to really begin to grow and accumulate a solid financial foundation.

WORKSHEET 106: PERSONAL ASSETS

	Name	Amount	
1	House	198,000.00	
2	Car - Camry	8,000.00	
3	Car - Buick	19,450.00	
4	Jewelry	2,500.00	
5	Cash in bank	14,000.00	
6	401 K	127,000.00	
7	Roth IRA	34,359.00	
8	College Fund	17,545.00	
9			
	Total	420,854.00	

WORKSHEET 107: PERSONAL LIABILITIES

	Name	Type S / L	Balance Owed	
1	Mortgage	L	143,000	
2	Camry Loan	L	4,300	
3	Buick Loan	L	14,500	
4	Credit Cards	S	17,000	
5				
6	Total		178,800	

WORKSHEET 108:
NET WORTH/EQUITY STATEMENT

Personal Financial Profile Assets	Current Value	Liabilities	Balance Owed	
Cash in Banks	14,000.00	Mortgages	143,000.00	
Real Estate Owned	198,000.00	Bank Loans		
Automobiles	27,450.00	Other Loans	18,800.00	
Jewelry	2,500.00	Bank Credit Cards	17,000.00	
Antiques		Bank Credit Cards		
401K	127,000.00	Bank Credit Cards		
Sep IRA / IRA		Bank Credit Cards		
Roth IRA	34,359.00	Dept. Store Cards		
Cash Value Life Insurance		Dept. Store Cards		
Stocks		Alimony / Child Sup		
Bonds		Misc. Liabilities		
Personal Profit Sharing		Misc. Liabilities		
Other Assets - college fund	17,545.00			
Other Assets		Total Liabilities	178,800.00	
Other Assets				
Other Assets		Total assets -	420,854.00	
Other Assets		Total Liabilities	178,800.00	
Total Assets	420,854.00	Net Worth	242,054.00	
	Purchase	Amount	Current	
Real Estate Owned	Price	Owed	Value	Equity
Your Residence	175,000	143,000.00	198,000.00	55,000.00
Other Real Estate				
Other Real Estate				
Total Real Estate Owned	175,000	143,000.00	198,000.00	55,000.00
Vehicles Owned	25,000.00	4,300.00	8,000.00	3,700.00
Vehicles Owned	22,500.00	14,500.00	19,450.00	4,950.00
Vehicles Owned				
Vehicles Owned				
Total Vehicles Owned	47,500.00	18,800.00	27,450.00	8,650.00

CHAPTER 11:
CREATING YOUR DEBT REDUCTION AND SAVINGS PLAN

It's not so much how much you make as how much you save!

Interest on debt grows without rain.
– Yiddish Proverb

When sitting down with people, we will often find that once they have made all the cuts possible in their spending, and they have their living budget in place, they will still often struggle to free up even a small amount of extra income to put into a savings/investing plan. So, depending on the amount of disposable income available, we recommend that people begin with "percent bites."

For example, instead of saying someone needs to save 10 percent of his or her available income right away—$100 of every $1,000 of income—an amount that can seem daunting to a lot of people, we recommend that people set a goal of putting a minimum of 3 percent into their financial management system, and live off of 97 percent of their income. The 3 percent can then be applied to their savings plan—$30 from $1,000. We then suggest they take 1 percent of that, or $10 from $1000, to apply to conservative/short-term savings, 1 percent to long-term savings/investing, and 1 percent to tithing/sharing. The next goal would be to increase the percentages over time.

Sabrina and I are firm believers of the phrase "Give it out in slices and it comes back in loaves." When people create a plan for giving and start applying that plan, they will often begin to see blessings come back in many forms. We have found that there is no greater feeling than doing something that benefits someone else's life and then seeing the impact of our positive influence.

* * * * *

One Christmas, Sabrina and I decided we were going to collect toys and bring them to a homeless shelter that took in women and children. We made the appropriate arrangements to go there on Christmas morning and hand out presents. The shelter gave us a list of how many toys they needed, plus a few extra. My daughter and I set out to collect the gifts.

The day before Christmas, we were still short of the number of toys we needed. It looked like we might need to go to the store and buy the rest. Cash was very tight at the time and I needed to use the money I had to make the lease payment on one of my limousines the following Friday. But we had promised the shelter that we would bring a toy for every child. After praying about the situation, I stepped out on a leap of faith. Sabrina and I went shopping and spent $397 for the toys we still needed.

The next morning, we brought the toys to the shelter. It was so gratifying to see the smiles on all those little faces when the kids opened up their presents.

The morning after Christmas, a letter showed up at our house. It was from a man I had provided limo service to three years prior. He had paid with a check that I hadn't been able to cash. I didn't think I would ever see the money again. The letter said, "We are so sorry for taking so long to pay you. We had to move away and didn't have the money to pay you. Things are better now, so here is the money owed for the limousine and a little more. We hope you have a Merry Christmas." Inside the letter was a check for $398!

* * * * *

The following pages will present a step-by-step system for creating a monthly spending, saving, sharing and debt reduction plan. It is designed to meet people of any income level and walk them through the process from getting out of debt and developing a savings/investment plan. This is the beginning to becoming financially independent.

To better illustrate this monthly savings plan, we're going to tell you a story of how a couple named John and Maryann Smith started to save and invest money, got out of debt, and began the journey to becoming financially independent.

When the Smiths first began implementing their plan, their monthly take-home income was $3,000. They were spending all they made and were even putting excess expenses on their credit cards.

When I first sat down with them, they told me that they wanted to save money. They knew they were spending more than they should, yet it seemed like there was always "more month at the end of their money." Their purchases included clothes, school supplies for their kids, and entertainment. They often had to put food, insurance, and their utilities on credit cards in order to pay their bills on time. John and Maryann were afraid of losing their jobs, because if they did, they wouldn't be able to make ends meet. They were living paycheck to paycheck and hated it. It was causing a lot of stress on their marriage, and they weren't able to do the things for their children they wished to.

They didn't think they would ever be able to retire, let alone be able to help their kids pay for college. When they first got married, John's father had told them the Golden Rule of Finance: "Pay yourself ten percent of all that you make." They thought it sounded good but didn't have enough to make ends meet as it was.

We sat and talked for a good couple of hours and they shared their frustrations with me. We talked about their goals and dreams, and what having money meant to them. I then told them that they had the ability to make their dreams and goals come true, and that they would be able to retire and even help their children pay for college if they wanted to. However; it would take a lot of work, time, and discipline to make regular deposits into their savings/investment accounts. I could see a sense of peace come over them, and they began to smile again.

The first thing I had them do was put together a budget or spending plan, as we already discussed in Chapter 5.

After going through their expenses, they discovered they were able to cut some things from their budget and free up some extra money. When we got back together, we went through their living budget and together, were able to find even more ways to reduce their monthly expenses, or cash outflow.

Insurance

One thing we looked at were their insurance policies. It turned out they had really low deductibles on their policies. I explained that many people will carry low deductibles because they are afraid of the potential out-of-pocket costs if something should happen. The lower the deductible, the higher the insurance premium.

Like most people, however, the Smiths didn't know that even if they had an accident or something happened to their house, their monthly premium could be hit with a 10-percent or higher surcharge that would remain on their policy for up to three years. Plus, insurance companies have a score, similar to a credit score, which will affect the cost of their insurance or even determine if they are able to get insurance.

This means that filing a claim for anything less than one thousand dollars could often cost more than they would get from the insurance company. I explained that they would be better off self-insuring the first thousand dollars and use their insurance for large claims. A great way to accomplish that is to create an insurance savings account and fund it over time until they have a thousand dollars in it.

The Smiths liked that idea, so I had them call their agent and raise the deductible to a thousand dollars, which reduced their insurance premiums by $30 a month.

Tax Exemptions

The Smiths told me they always get a tax refund at the end of the year for around $2,000. I had John Smith contact the personnel director where he works to increase the number of exemptions to reduce the amount of money taken out of his paycheck every month. John would have a smaller tax refund at the end of the year, but the family would have more money to use each month.

Eating Out
We also found that John was eating lunch out three to four times a week, so he agreed to bring a bag lunch instead, and only eat out once in a while.

Phone / Cable Plan
I also had John call his phone/cable company to negotiate a less expensive plan. Cable companies are always competing with each other, so if you call them and threaten to switch to one of their competitors, they will often give you a better deal in order to keep you as a customer.

By the time we were done with the first series of cuts, the Smiths had reduced their expenses to only 97 percent of their income.

Creating an Emergency Fund
We then talked about how part of why they didn't feel financially secure was because they didn't have an emergency fund in place. When something happened, they would whip out their credit cards to cover it, increasing their debt load.

As they began to work on their monthly savings plan, they would be able to add to their emergency fund and their debt load would begin to shrink.

I explained that the challenge of not having an emergency fund in place was that if they didn't have any money set aside in case of an emergency, then life would at times seem like a string of emergencies. I then recommended that an emergency fund be the first area they build up. They should accumulate enough savings to cover at least three months, and ideally six months, of their current monthly living expenses.

I have found that if people don't have at least three months of living expenses set aside in an emergency fund, they are continually playing catch up. Or, as we like to say, referring to Murphy's

Law: "If you invite Murphy, he won't show up. But when you're not ready, he is sure to come."

John and Maryann started to put any extra money into their emergency fund, and then went to work on reducing their short-term debt. After going through John and Maryann's debts, I suggested that they start to save money and pay down their debt at the same time.

It is important to apply money toward debt reduction and a portion toward savings at the same time. The two need to go hand in hand. We find that many people will either save money or pay down their debt. However; few will do both at the same time.

By staying true to their plan, the Smiths will become disciplined in saving money and begin the journey to reaching financial freedom. If they stay consistent with their plan, it will start to take on energy of its own. John and Maryann will start to see their savings begin to grow and their debt begin to disappear.

Liquid Assets

The next time we got together, I told them that a good goal to work toward would be to have at least one year of expenses in various accounts that are easily assessable or liquid, just in case something happens and they need to access to them. There is no greater feeling than to know you could go a year without any income coming in and you would be all right financially.

Options for places to put savings are:

• Six months of expenses in a passbook savings account or money market account for emergencies
• Then six months' worth of expenses in an account or investments that yield a little better return, safe from potential risk, and is very conservative.

Once John and Maryann have their emergency funds in place, are paying themselves first every time they get paid, consistently applying money towards: expenses, short-term, mid-term, and

Long-term savings, and charity/tithing, we recommend that they start to increase the percentages.

John, Maryann, and I met two weeks later to fine-tune their plan and to discuss their progress. They were coming along wonderfully and staying disciplined to their plan. So, I recommended that they keep working on reducing their expenses and set a goal to get their living expenses down to 90 percent of their income within the next three months.

For some people, getting their expenses down to 90 percent of their income can take one or two months. It might take others as long as six months. We would recommend, however, that you

try to reach the point where you are living on 90 percent of your income within the first three months of implementing this money management system.

John and Maryann were starting to feel more comfortable with this system. I recommend that they start to build up the percentages they applied for charity/tithing to 10 percent as quickly as possible. They would feel good being able to help others.

I shared with them how, when we are able to help others, our self-confidence increases dramatically. It is from the process of putting the systems into place and having the discipline to develop a strong savings plan that we are able to start developing a wealth-oriented mindset.

After two and a half months, John and Maryann were living on only 90 percent of what they were making and applying 10 percent to their money management system. We got back together for a progress check, and I even brought them a cake to celebrate their accomplishments.

After we celebrated, I recommended that a good mid- to long-term goal would be to increase their savings/investing and sharing to the point where they were living on only 70 percent of what they made, and applying 30 percent to their plan. For most people, depending on where they are at financially, this may take a while. And that's okay, for that is the mid- to long-term goal.

After going back through their budget and expenses, Maryann told me that she always wanted to start a small business and that one of her friends had a small e-commerce business. Her friend had told Maryann that she would help her start one as well if she wanted. Maryann asked me if I thought that was a good idea. I told her to do more research about the business idea and put together a business plan. We would get back together in a week and I would review it for her.

I continued to meet with John and Maryann once a quarter for a check-up to make share they were staying on track. It took some time, but John and Maryann reached the point where they were living on only 70 percent of what they made and saving, sharing, and investing the rest. They had set the goal to reach that point and they finally made it.

Maryann called me and said, "We did it, we did it! We finally reached our goal. We are now able to put 30 percent of what we make back into our financial plan."

"That's fantastic, Maryann," I said. "I knew you to would get there. How does it feel?"

"It feels amazing. John and I now know that we will be able to reach the other goals that we have. In fact, we can't wait until we are able to check off becoming debt-free as well," Maryann said, giggling.

"Well, Maryann, you just made my day. I would like to take you and John out for dinner to celebrate. How does next Friday look for you two?"

"Friday looks great," Maryann responded.

Friday evening came, and we had a wonderful dinner. After dinner, while we were eating dessert, we went back over their goals and further discussed their beliefs about money. I suggested that since they were now living on only 70 percent of what they made, they now allocate 10 percent to charity or tithing, 10 percent toward short-term, more conservative savings/ investments, and 10 percent to mid- or long-range investing toward retirement.

I explained that the degree of aggressiveness at which they invest for the long term depends on their age and risk tolerance and tends to be different for everyone. There are many compo- nents that go into the investment mix and any investments should ideally be reviewed at least quarterly and if not quarterly, every six months to one year at the bare minimum.

It is important to develop a working relationship with a good financial advisor, one who has the experience to deal with many different situations yet is able to have a holistic or comprehensive approach. An advisor should be able to put his or her clients' needs first yet have access to a wide range of solutions with which to work.

I told John and Maryann how important it is to have an advisor with a long-term perspective to help them create and stay on track with their financial plan. Their advisor should sit down with them to create a list of goals, help them stay on track, continue to monitor their current situation, and determine the best course of action to take according to their goals.

Maryann said smiling, "We know, Mike. That is why we are so thankful for having you in our corner. You have helped make the process of saving money, getting out of debt, and investing for the future so much easier. Thanks to all your help, we now know that we will be all right financially."

"Thank you, John and Maryann. You are very kind. I am really glad to be a trusted advisor for you and that I'm able to help you two reach your financial goals. I know that you two have been working on your money management system for a while now and have been making great progress." I responded, smiling.

Two Different Scenarios for Building Net Worth

Sabrina and I are now going to walk you through two different scenarios, one without short-term debt, one with short-term debt. We are going to use John and Maryann situation as an example to show you how the process works. Both scenarios start with a monthly combined take-home pay of $4,500 and their living on 97% of that take-home pay, 1% sharing/tithing, 1% for short-term savings, and 1% for long-term savings.

Scenario #1 (no short-term debt):
$4,500 = Take-home pay
97% = $4,365 to cover living expenses 1% = $45 to charity
1% = $45 to short-term savings
1% = $450 to long-term savings/investments

Short-term savings tend to be more liquid, or easily converted to cash if you need it. Long-term savings are those that go toward investments with terms over one year.

As we discussed earlier, if you don't have an emergency fund in place, we recommend that the first thing you do is to build up that fund to cover all your expenses for three to six months. Until you get your emergency fund in place and funded, the amount you would normally apply to short-term savings and long-term investing should be put into your emergency fund. In our example, that would be $13,095 ($4,365 x 3 months), or better yet, six months, $26,190 ($4,365 x 6 months).

If your monthly expenses go up or down, we recommend that you adjust your emergency fund accordingly. Let's say that your monthly expenses were $3,800 instead of $4,365, then you would only need $11,400 ($3,800 x 3 months) to $22,800 ($3,800 x 6 months) in your emergency fund.

If your monthly outgoing expenses are $4,365 and you apply 1 percent toward charity/tithing, and 2 percent to short- and long-term savings, at the end of three months, your accounts should look like this:

Money set aside for charity: $45 x 3 = $135 Money set aside for savings: $90 x 3 = $270

After working this system for three months, let's assume that you have your budget in place and you are now spending only 90 percent of what you make. You are now able to apply 10 percent to your savings plan. At this point, we recommend that you decide how you want to build up the amount you share/tithe until you reach 10 percent.

Scenario #1.after three months, John and Maryann were able to reduce Plan

Because it's so important that you have your emergency fund in place, we recommend that you raise the amount you apply to sharing/tithing equally to the other two parts: 3 percent charity, 3.5 percent short-term savings, and percent 3.5 long-term savings. This is what it would look like:

$4,500 = Monthly take-home pay
90% = $4,050 to cover living expenses
10% of $4,500 = $450 to apply to charity/tithing and savings.

3% = $135 to charity
3.5 % = $157.50 to short-term savings
3.5 % = $157.50 to long-term savings/investments

At the end of nine months, your savings should look like this:

Money set aside for charity: Months 1 to 3: $45 x 3 = $135
Months 3 to 12: $135 x 9 = $1,215 Total at the end of nine months:
$135 + 1,215 = $1,350

Money set aside for savings:
Months 1 to 3: $90 x 3 = $270
Months 3 to 12: $157.50 x 9 = $1,417.50 Total at the end of nine months:
$270 + $1,417.50 = $1,552.50

This is the foundation upon which you will begin your climb to financial independence.

Financial Independence:
The point at which you have enough passive income to pay for your desired standard of living.

Scenario #2 (with short-term debt):
So what happens if you have short-term debt? These are debts that you would normally pay off within one year, such as credit card debt. In this case, split the amount you are putting into savings, and pay one-half toward short-term savings or paying off your short-term debt, instead of putting this money into long-term savings/investing.

Again, let's look at John and Maryann's situation, as an example to illustrate the process. When they first started, they did not have an emergency fund in place. We therefore set a goal of creating a fund that would cover six months of their living expenses. John and Maryann also owed $13,500 in credit card debt and had a car loan of $8,500, with a combined debt balance of $22,000. They set a goal of paying off that debt in five years. Given their current financial situation, we recommended applying their percentages as follows:

$4,500 = Combined take-home pay 97% = $4,365 to cover living expenses 1% = $45 to charity
1% = $45 to short-term savings
1% = $45 to paying off short-term debt

Depending on your debt load and personal belief system, you decide how quickly or slowly you increase the amount you put toward sharing or tithing. For the purpose of this exercise; however, we are going to keep the numbers the same as in Scenario 1. After three months, the numbers would look like this:
$45 x 3 = $135 to charity/tithing
$45 x 3 = $135 to short-term savings
$45 x 3 = $135 to short-term debt reduction

Continue using this formula until your short-term debt is paid off.

* * * * *

To help illustrate this system, let's follow John and Maryann Smith and watch their progress over the course of one year. As in their monthly expenses to 90 percent of their take-home pay, allowing them to apply 30% to charity, 3.5 percent to short- term savings, and this time, apply 3.5 percent to short-term debt reduction.

By the beginning of Year 2, John and Maryann were bringing home $4,700 a month and living on 80 percent of their income, or $3,760. Of the remaining 20 percent, they decided to bump up the percentage given to charity to 6 percent of their take-home pay, or $282, short-term savings to 7 percent, or $329, and increase the percentage that went to debt reduction or long-term savings/ investment to 7 percent, or $329 as well.

We recommended that the Smiths continue to apply $329 to reducing their short-term debt until it was completely paid off. After that, the 7 percent could be applied to long-term savings or investments.

Going into year 3, the Smiths are earning $4,900 combined per month and living on only 70 percent of their income, or $3,430. Now they are able to increase the amount they donate to charitable causes or tithing to 10 percent, or $490 per month, 10percent, or $490, to short-term savings, and 10 percent, or $490, to debt reduction or long-term savings/investments

Even though they are making more money per month, the Smiths were able to reduce their monthly living expenses by following their monthly savings plan. This also means that they could reduce the amount of money in their emergency fund from$13,095 (3 months x $4,365)   to $10,290 or $26,190 (6 months x $4,365) to $20, 540.

As you can see, you can speed up your wealth accumulation process by either reducing your expenses, increasing your income or by doing both.

In Year 4, Maryann's boss was so happy with her work that he gave her a raise and a year-end bonus of $5,000. The Smith's take-home pay is now $5,200 a month. They continue living on 70 percent of their take-home pay, or $3,640, setting aside 10 percent, or $520, each for donations, short-term savings, and long-term investments. What should the Smiths decide to do with the bonus? Should they go on a trip or buy the long-awaited dining room set they've been admiring at the mall?

John and Maryann remembered our conversation about funding their emergency fund before they did anything else. They also recalled that following their monthly savings plan would take time, discipline, and hard work. As long as they stayed faithful to their plan, I recommended that they celebrate their successes by taking a small amount out of their budget to acknowledge their achievements. It's important to acknowledge and celebrate successes to stay motivated.

Over a romantic dinner at a nice restaurant, John and Maryann decided to take $500, or 10 percent of the $5,000 bonus to take a short trip with their kids. They would then put the rest of the bonus into their emergency fund. The Smith's dedication and commitment paid off. At the end of Year 4,

One day, my phone rang, and it was Maryann.

"Mike, we did it! We did it!" I could hear her excitement over the phone.

"What did you do?" I asked.

"We finally fully funded our emergency fund and we have money left over. Right now, we are only spending $3,640 a month and have $22,120 in our short-term savings account. That's enough to cover six months of our living expenses!" she explained.

"Wow, that's great! You and John should be very proud.

How's your debt reduction coming along?

"We have paid our short-term debt down by $17,620.50 and only have $4,379.50 left to go," she told me, still excited.

"Wonderful, Maryann. You two will have that paid down in no time," I said.

"I know. I can't wait. It feels like we have been paying things off forever," she said.

"Remember, I told you and John when we first met that this would take time. You two are doing really well. I'm proud of you for sticking to your savings plan. Keep up the great work!"

The Smiths continued their debt reduction plan with the goal of being debt-free except for their mortgage within five years. They discussed how they had been able to pay off their entire credit card debt, then roll those payments into their car loan. They paid the car loan off in nine months into Year 5, allowing them to reach their goal. After meeting with them, we went out to lunch to celebrate.

* * * * *

Time, Patience, and Perseverance

As you can see from John and Maryann's story, it can take a while to build an emergency fund, pay off short-term debt, and move into long-term saving and/or investing. It took the Smiths four years to save up six months' of living expenses in their emergency fund, and five years to pay off all their short-term debt. How quickly you are able to get control of your financial future depends on how you much you can reduce your expenses and/or how quickly you can increase your income.

Building up savings takes time, so you need to remain patient through the process. Some of the challenges include the extent to which you can reduce your expenses. If you are employed, the degree to which you can increase your take-home pay may be limited as well. One way to acquire more money for savings, reducing your expenses, helping other people, and produce an additional income stream is opening a small business you can do around your job. You have probably heard the phrase, "Don't quit your day job." This only holds true until your own business or investments reach a point at which they bring in more money than your job does. This does not mean looking for get-rich-quick schemes. Know that building your investments to the point of being able to live on the interest takes time. Remember that you're in control of how fast your savings grow. With time and discipline, when you keep funding your financial plan month after month, you will eventually become financially independent.

"You must gain control over your money or the lack of it will forever control you."
— Dave Ramsey

CHAPTER 12:
BECOMING DEBT-FREE

The trick to creating wealth is to separate your bad debt from your good debt, then go to work on eliminating your bad debt!

his chapter offers a great system for reducing or paying down short-term debt. Some people will pay off their credit card or a short-term loan, and then put the "extra" money back into their budget to spend.

People often ask us, "If I start applying a percentage of what I am making to paying down my debt, what do I pay off first?" or "Do I just pay the minimum payments, or do I pay more?" or "When I pay off this credit card, do I just cut it up?" There are many answers to these questions and what follows is meant to provide some guidelines for reducing and eliminating your debt.

Eliminating Your Debt

The trick to paying off debt is making your progress fun and easy to follow consistently—consistently being the key word. You will begin to pick up momentum as you start to pay off one credit card, then the next, and the next.

The system works like this: First, organize your short-term debt in order of amount owed, from the lowest balance to the highest balance. Some financial advisors recommend ranking your short-term debts by the highest interest rate to the lowest. Granted, that makes sense financially, because you'll be reducing the amount of interest you pay. However, we would like to show you a different way to look at reducing debts.

If you have four credit cards and the card with the highest interest rate has the highest balance, you will be paying toward the card for a long time and it won't feel like you're getting anywhere.

However, if you rank the cards by the lowest balance amount first, you will be able to pay the first card off sooner, which will give you a great sense of accomplishment.

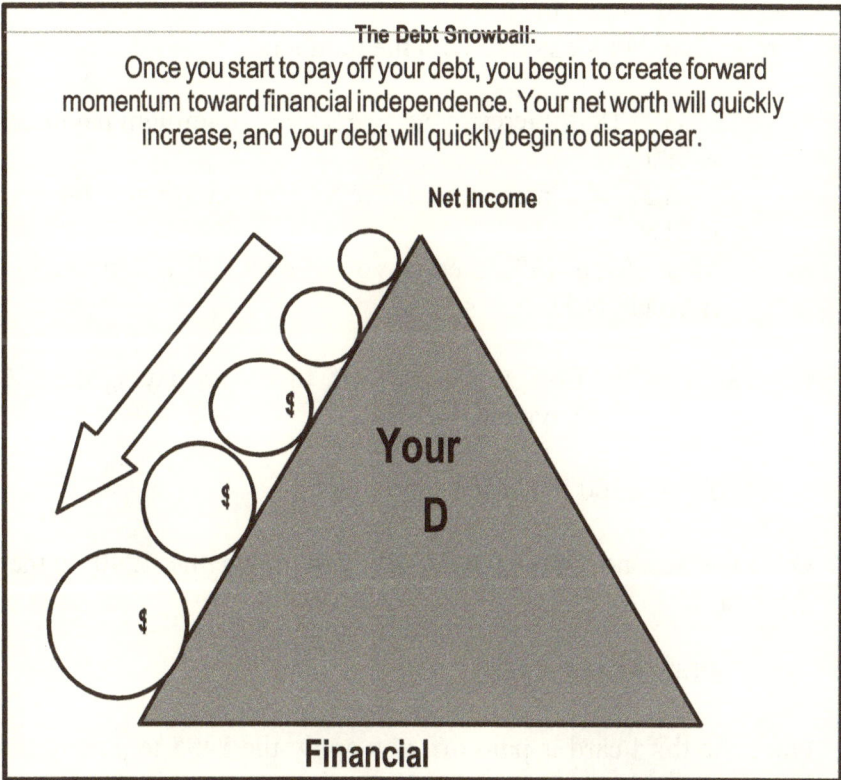

The Debt Snowball:
Once you start to pay off your debt, you begin to create forward momentum toward financial independence. Your net worth will quickly increase, and your debt will quickly begin to disappear.

Net Income

Your

D

Financial

Becoming Debt-Free

You then transfer the payment from the first card to the card with the next lowest balance. Simply follow the process to the next card and the next card until all your cards are paid off.

Once your credit cards are paid off, transfer the amount you were paying toward the cards to any longer term or mid-term debt you may have, such as a car loan. Once the car loan is paid off, then apply the payments toward other long-term debt or your mortgage.

This system is referred to as the "debt snowball." It works like a snowball rolling down a hill. While the "snowball" might start at a very low amount, like your "minimum payment," it will pick up size as it rolls down the hill.

Here's what that looks like with the numbers:

- Visa 1: 18% interest, you owe $3,000, minimum payment is $80
- Visa 2: 14% interest, you owe $4,500, minimum payment is $160
- MasterCard: 17% interest, you owe $6,000, minimum payment is $165.

Pay $80 until the first card is paid off, then start paying the $80 plus the minimum payment on Visa 2:

$$\$80 + \$160 = \$240$$

Once the second card is paid off, you move the $240 to the third card:

$$\$240 + \$165 = \$405$$

Once the third card is paid off, you apply the $405 to paying off long-term debt

When you begin the process, continue to pay at least the minimum due on each card, then try to pay more toward the card with the lowest balance when you can. Pay the minimum due on each card every month and try to pay more toward the card with the highest interest rate when you can. The trick is to apply all available money towards one card or loan payment at a time while paying the minimum on the other cards. To better illustrate this, look at the cart on the next page.

Visa #1	Visa #2	MasterCard
18% interest Balance (amount you owe): $3,000 Minimum payment: $80	14% interest Balance: $4,500 Minimum payment: $160	17% interest Rate Balance: $6,000 Minimum payment: $165
Pay off the first card, then move the $80 payment to the second card.	$80 $160 $240 Once the second card is paid off, then apply the $240 to the third card.	$240 $165 $405 Once the third card is paid off, move the $405 to other mid – or - long-term debt.

Now let's look at paying off that car loan:

Loan balance: $8,500
Monthly loan payment: $350
Amount now available because credit cards
are paid off: $405 + $385 = $755

Use the $775 to pay off your car loan. Then move the $755 to the next loan until all short-term, mid-term, and long-term debts are paid off. Once you are able to start applying extra money toward your financial management system, as John and Maryann Smith did, apply the amount targeted for debt reduction to pay   off the card with the lowest balance, just as the debt snowball illustrates..

As you can see, by transferring one payment on a credit card to the next payment, you will gain momentum and you will be able to pay off your debts more quickly. Before you know it, your debts are eliminated.

When you are able to transfer that "extra" amount into your savings/investment plan, your wealth creation will begin to really take off and you can start moving in the direction of your dreams. Congratulations!!!

You have paid off all your debt except for your mortgage. Some common questions we're often asked is: "Should I apply the money I have been paying toward eliminating my debt toward paying my mortgage off early?" Or "Should I apply the money I've been paying toward debt towards my retirement/wealth accumulation plan?" We believe you need to do both. Once your short-term and mid-term debt is gone, we recommend that you apply as much as you comfortably can toward your retirement/ wealth accumulation plan.

The real question is how fast you should pay off your mortgage. Some people feel they are more comfortable paying off their mortgage early. For many people, owning their house completely free and clear brings with it a great peace of mind, and is a good goal. However, paying off your mortgage early doesn't always make the most financial sense.

On the surface, paying off your mortgage early sounds great, if you have enough money coming in each month to be able to still fund your retirement. If you pay more toward your mortgage, you may not have enough extra money to invest toward retire- ment. Having your house free and clear makes your house your largest financial asset, but you may not be able to access the money if you need to. We refer to this as being land rich and cash poor. This could be a bad place to be if you want to keep living in your house moving into retirement.

If the interest rate on your mortgage is very low, you may be able to find a better place to invest your money. We call this opportunity cost, or the cost of choosing one thing over another.

Another risk to making extra mortgage payments is that if you were to lose your job and needed to access the equity in your house, you probably wouldn't able to. Without a job, the bank won't give you a loan, even if you have already paid off most of the mortgage and you only owe a small amount. In addition, if for some reason, you're not able to make the mortgage payment, you could face the risk of going into foreclosure.

All that said, there is a great trick for paying off your mortgage early and only paying a little bit more then you would otherwise have to pay. Instead of paying your mortgage once a month as you normally would, make your mortgage payment every two weeks. This is done by telling your lender that your want to make bi-weekly payments, or half the mortgage in the first two weeks, and half the mortgage payment two weeks later. That way, you end up making one extra payment each year, which will allow you to pay off your mortgage in 23 years instead of 30.

Another train of thought is rather than making extra pay- ments on your mortgage, you invest the money in a long-term savings/investment account that yields more interest than you're paying on your mortgage. This money would be liquid, or more readily available. In this way, your money would grow more quickly than it would if you were paying off the mortgage. Plus you would remain in control of the money. As the long-term savings/investment account grows, you would be able to withdraw money from that account and pay off your mortgage if you chose to.

When it comes to deciding if you should pay your mortgage off early instead of applying available cash flow to your retire-ment or wealth creation plan, there are many different variables within your overall financial picture. We therefore highly recommend that you take a close look at your goals, your current financial condition, and your overall financial plan. Then, after discussing your plan with your financial advisor, decide which method is the best fit for what you're trying to accomplish, and which option best fits your financial situation and risk comfort level

The difference between the
rich and the poor is:
the rich invest their money
and spend what's left,
and the poor spend their
money and invest what's left.
—Jim Rohn

Wealth is a mindset; so is poverty,what you know or don't know, your perspective of life and beliefs have a direct connection to you net worth – Dr. Lucas D Shallua

HAPTER 13:
GROWING YOUR NET WORTH

All fortunes begin with a sound plan and the discipline to stay on track!

We started out by having you create a living budget and talked about why it's important to plan your expenses around your lifestyle. We showed you some great ways to purge your expenses so you can free up extra cash that can be used to invest. We also explained the importance of having an emergency fund. Then you created a net worth statement and listed all your assets and liabilities.

Once you created a living budget and net worth statement and you knew what your net worth was, we walked you through a detailed process for paying off your short-term, mid-term, and long-term debt. We also talked about whether or not it makes sense to pay your mortgage off early. Now comes the fun part: wealth creation.

By now, you are able to consistently invest money into your financial plan. If you haven't yet, this is the point where you may want to sit down with a financial professional or an investment advisor and put together a comprehensive financial plan.

When you design your plan, it's very important that you create a plan that works around your lifestyle. As things in your life change, you will want to make the necessary adjustments to your plan. There are many different rules and limitations that apply to different investments, so please contact your financial advisor or tax professional for the most current strategies or programs.

When setting up your retirement plan, it's very important to set a goal to fully fund the maximum amount you're able to contribute. That said, it's better to start by funding less and doing it more often. As with everything else, the more consistent you are with your savings/investing, the easier it will become.

For the Self-Employed

If you are self-employed, we would suggest that you pay yourself a salary that covers your living expenses, charity, and other investments. It's very important, however, that this money management system be treated as a business expense. As a business owner, your goal is to get to the point where your salary is lower than your net business income.

For example, let's say your business brings in a monthly gross income of $10,000. Your monthly business operating expenses are $4,000. Therefore, your business's net monthly income is $6,000. Pay yourself a salary of $5,000. This means you have a surplus in your business of $1,000

That is when your business will start helping you build your wealth. It can also start to get tricky, because you want to pay yourself enough to cover your living expenses, have enough extra for charity, and to invest in your retirement plan. You still need to make sure you keep enough working capital in the business to maintain a strong cash flow for your business.

As you complete the budget for your business, you need to track your business expenses. You may also want to put a percentage aside for charity, and it's a good idea to create and apply a percentage towards a business saving/investing account. In essence, you would follow the same system for your business as you do for your personal financial management system. Treat your business as if it were an independent person separate from yourself. The job of the business is to support you. However, I would suggest that you also treat your business a member of the community. As you did for your personal budget, go to the www.childrenandbeyond.com website and download the spread-sheets for preparing your business budget.

For your business, we recommend that you use the following formula. a good rule of thumb is to keep your operating expenses around 30 percent of your gross revenue. If at all possible, set the goal of keeping the remainder of your expenses, including your salary, between 40 and 50 percent of your gross revenue.

For the sake of illustration, we are going to assume that your business expenses are 70 percent of your gross revenue, leaving a net profit of 30 percent. You would then take the 30 percent profit and apply it to your business's financial management system.

We recommend that you take the 30 percent and divide it up this way: 10 percent of your net income, or 10 percent of the 30. percent profit and apply it to charity. We have found that it is equally beneficial to businesses to give back to the community. Plus, charitable contributions are often tax deductible, which can positively affect your tax situation. When making contributions, we suggest getting the opinion of a tax professional.

Some businesspeople take 10 percent of their gross revenue and apply it toward tithing or charity. This can be very daunting to people, particularly new business owners and start-ups. It will likely be easier to commit to 10 percent of your net business revenue. As a business owner, this is a personal decision, so go with what best fits your beliefs and your business plan.

Then apply 30 percent of your net business profit toward short-term savings, business debt reduction, or your business emergency fund. Just as with your personal finances, it's a good idea to have three to six months of business expenses set aside for emergencies in a savings account. Put 30 percent of your net revenue into long-term savings/investments or debt reduction, and then 30 percent reinvested in your business.

Remember, there are two kinds of debt: good debt and bad debt. Good debt is when you borrow money to acquire an asset that helps you earn more money. For instance, I borrowed $50,000 to purchase a limousine. My monthly payments were $1,500, but the limousine on average, brought in $5,000 per month in income. Without borrowing the money, I wouldn't have been able to buy the limousine, and therefore couldn't have earned the $3,500.

On the other hand, an example of bad debt would be when I ran up $10,000 on a credit card to buy office furniture and equipment for a real estate office I wanted to open. At the time, I didn't have any agents to help me or the time to sell enough houses to pay off the debt. Within six months, I had to move out of the office and put the furniture in storage, leaving me with debts of $15,000.

Keep in mind that when developing the financial plan for your business, these percentages can increase or decrease, depending on the type of business and your business goals. We recommend that you consult your tax professional and financial advisor as you are creating your plan.

Here is an example of how the numbers would look using the above scenario:

Monthly gross income from the business:	$10,000
Monthly operating expenses:	$ 3,000
Salary:	$ 4,000
Monthly Net Income:	$ 7,000

Monthly net expenses and salary are
70 percent of gross income

Remaining monthly net income:	$ 3,000
10% to charity	$ 300
30% to short-term savings, debt reduction	$ 900
30% to long-term savings/investing	$ 900
30% to reinvesting in the business	$ 900
	$ 3,000

As we mentioned above, when you truly put a system in place for creating wealth, the most important component of that system is the consistency with which you put the various steps into place, coupled with the discipline of following them every day. This is where your plan starts to take on a life of its own.

Even something as small as consistently adding $1 to your savings/investment plan, over time, will turn into a fortune if this is done each and every day. When you consistently divide your income up into the three parts, spending, saving, and sharing, your financial state will start to improve. Unfortunately, most people are too busy looking for ways to make a lot of money, and miss out on the little things that will over time turn into a fortune. As Jim Rohn says, "Wealth is created from our savings, not our earnings."

Let's illustrate with a story about Mr. Smith, an old farmer who always dreamed of finding a large diamond. He would feed his animals and quickly plow his fields. He went around the countryside looking for diamonds day in and day out, until one day he got frustrated and quit farming. Mr. Smith sold his farm and went out searching for diamonds. He went through diamond mine after diamond mine until he was too old to dig any more.

One morning, Mr. Smith picked up a newspaper and saw an article about a guy who discovered the largest diamond ever found. To Mr. Smith's surprise, the gentlemen found the diamond while he was plowing his field, preparing to plant his spring crops. He was the very same gentlemen who bought Mr. Smith's farm. Mr. Smith had gone out searching for diamonds, yet had lived right on top of the largest diamond around, and never saw it because he was too busy looking in other places.

Like Mr. Smith, many people say they want to become a millionaire or make a lot of money, yet they will move from one get-rich-quick idea to another. Or they will spend their weekly or monthly salary as soon as it comes in, regardless of if it is $500 or $10,000, not saving anything for later is where they run in trouble.

A great way to earn more income or increase your current salary is to find something and leave it better than you found it, or help people solve their problems. It could be a product or service. Look around and find something that's broken and fix it or find a service that could be done better and improve upon it. If you continue to give back to society, and bring in new and improved products and services, your own value will improve. Then keep tabs on your money.

In my own business, I should have known that we were headed towards financial trouble when Jennifer, my wife, asked me how much money we were spending, and I answered, "I'm not sure. Not much." The scary part was that I thought I had a pretty good handle on our finances. It wasn't until I finally sat down and did a living budget that I realized we were actually upside down without realizing it.

As we discussed in Chapter Three, it's very important that while you begin to build a strong financial foundation, you also need to grow yourself. There are different levels that you will need to move through. And if you skip any of those levels, your foundation will not become as strong. It makes no sense to build a beautiful house if the foundation is made of sand.

My problem lies in reconciling my gross habits with my net income.
– Errol Flynn

Your net worth can fluctuate, but your self-worth should only appreciate. – Chris Gardner

CHAPTER 14:

PROTECTING YOUR NET WORTH

Building a fortune without the proper protection is like building your house on sand!

When it comes to investing, sometimes the best money you can make is the money you don't lose.

—Warren Buffett

It's important to keep an even balance between safety and financial growth. In this chapter, we will talk about ways to protect your assets. A great visual for creating your wealth creation plan is the process of building a house.

The first thing you do when you start to build a house is to have a plan, perhaps an architect's drawing, to know what your house is going to look like. Then you lay the foundation. The foundation on a house is similar to your financial plan, which is why it's so important to have a comprehensive financial plan, even if you're just starting out. The more detailed the plan, the stronger the foundation will be.

Next, you frame the outside of the house. You need to choose the materials that will best suit your house and provide stability and beauty. This would be the equivalent of establishing your timeline, short-term, mid-term, and long-term goals, and selecting the best vehicles or strategies to accomplish those goals.

After your house is framed and your exterior walls are in place, you put the roof on the house, so that you can protect the house from the different elements that could damage the house. When creating your financial plan, this is equivalent to making sure you have proper protection (insurance) in place to protect you from unforeseen catastrophes.

The final step to building your house would be to lay out the rooms and add the finishing touches. For your financial house, that would mean putting your current assets into the plan and planning out what future assets will go where.

If you build a house with a solid foundation and follow the proper steps when building it, the house will stand strong and become a safe environment for you to raise your family. If you design your financial plan properly, it will also stand strong and allow you to create the wealth you and your family deserve.

The hard part of building a house is its design and actual construction. However, once it's built and you move in, you still have to maintain it and make changes to it as time passes. The same is true with your financial plan. That's why it's so important that you have a strong relationship with a financial advisor who can sit down with you on an ongoing basis and help you make any necessary adjustments to your financial plan.

Let's focus on the roof over your financial house for a minute: your insurance. It's important to have proper protection.
You need to have enough insurance to protect your current assets, as well as enough to cover any liabilities you may have, as well as any really important future goals, such as paying for college. If you don't have the proper protection in place, then you are at risk of losing everything you have worked so hard for. One of the best definitions of insurance we've heard is: "Insurance is the transference of risk to an organization that's in the risk acceptance or risk management business."
Although it's important for you to have the proper amount of protection in place, you don't want to be over-protected or spend too much on insurance. When most people start out building their financial foundation, they don't have many assets and usually not a lot of money. So heaven forbid, if something catastrophic happens, they don't have a lot to lose—they just need the basic necessities. The basic insurance coverage everyone should start out with are:

- Auto insurance – if you drive or own a car
- Homeowner's insurance – if you own a house
- Renter's insurance – if you are renting
- Health insurance – at least major medical insurance

If you don't have health insurance through your job, there are some high deductible plans that are relatively inexpensive. As an example, our health insurance for a family of five is $550 per month.

As your financial life becomes more stable, and you start to acquire some assets or you begin to grow your family, start to increase your insurance coverage to properly protect the increase in your assets. At the same time, once your emergency fund is in place, you can create a savings account that will operate as a personal insurance account for you to use as a way of self-insuring yourself, at least to the level of your deductible. If your deductible is $1,000, for instance, then create a side account in which you keep $1,000, as we discussed with John and Maryann Smith earlier in the book. A good goal is to build your insurance account to the point that you can comfortably begin to increase the deductibles on your auto, home/rental policies, and even your health insurance.

> A deductible on your insurance is the amount you need to pay out of pocket when you file a claim with your insurance company.

Most insurance policies have a minimum deductible of $250, then move to a $500 deductible, then $1,000. If there is no way you could come up with $500 if you needed to, then start out with a $250 deductible. We would recommend starting out with a $500 deductible, even if you have to put the deductible on a credit card if something happens. Unfortunately, when you file an insurance claim, your policy will usually increase with a minimum of a 10% increase. So if a claim is under $500 or even $1,000, it would not be worth filing it.

Once you have at least $1,000 saved up in your personal insurance account. Increase all your deductibles to $1,000. You should begin to see a fairly large savings on your insurance policies once all your deductibles are at $1,000 or higher.

At this point, as you increase your insurance coverage to protect the increase in your assets, or if you have children, you may want to add these additional areas of insurance coverage.

- Life Insurance: Enough to cover your short-, mid- and long-
  term goals, and ideally enough to cover your
  family's current standard of living.
- Disability Insurance: Enough to cover your monthly living expenses.
- Long-term Care Insurance: Look into this type of insurance
  if you're over 50 and you have assets that are between $100,000 and $500,000. If your health declines to the point that you can no longer care for yourself and need to go into assisted living, you will need to spend down or pay all expenses until your net worth is $2,500 before Medicare kicks in. You could spend your life saving and investing, and without the proper protection in place, you could lose everything. Assisted living can cost between $80,000 and $100,000 a year out of pocket.

If your net worth is less than $100,000 and you need to spend that down before Medicare kicked in, your estate would take a hit. However, if your net worth is $450,000, and that amount needed to be spent down, the hit to your estate would be much more significant. This can be compared to the cost of long-term care insurance or proper protection. People with net worth of $500,000 or more are even more vulnerable to having their estates depleted.

The greatest vulnerability lies between a net worth of $100,000 and $500,000.

As your financial foundation becomes more stable and you are able to start implementing more of your larger goals, you can

really start to enjoy your ideal lifestyle. This is the point at which, all your hard work and discipline really start to pay off.

Passive Income

Passive income is income from an investment that comes passively from the investment itself in the form of dividends or interest.

Once the passive income from your investments or assets is at a point where there are enough revenues to cover your current lifestyle, you are very close to being financial independent. You may be able to eliminate disability insurance because you may no longer need it. Remember that the definition of financial independence is when your passive income covers your desired lifestyle.

Once you're at this point in your plan, you should be able to really think about what your vision of success is. What do you want to accomplish in life? Where do you want to direct your energy? This is where you will be able to focus on your passion or strong points. This is probably the most important part of the whole process, because as you move through this process, you will keep growing internally as you continue to put the steps in place to maintain and strengthen your financial foundation.

If you fall short during this phase, or skip too quickly through the process, you may start to lose traction and end up going backwards instead. For example, if a person saves a lot of money and ends up getting sick; but doesn't have health insurance, he or she could end up spending a good part of the money they worked so hard for, if not all of their savings, on medical expenses. That person would end up having to start all over again.

If you have teenaged children who are driving, or a business that is somewhat risky, we would recommend that you get a

$1 million balloon policy as part of your homeowner's coverage. We knew a man who ran a very successful business and shortly after he retired, his 16-year-old daughter tragically hit and killed a pedestrian. After a lengthy lawsuit, the man lost

everything because he didn't have adequate insurance.

Bad things can happen to good people, so it's very important to have proper coverage for your current situation. We would recommend that as part of your annual financial review, you have someone review your current insurance coverage as well.

Here are the basic components you should have in place to truly have a rock-solid financial foundation:

- A comprehensive wealth creation/retirement plan
- Consistent positive net cash flow
- Consistent positive net worth
- A good health insurance policy
- A life insurance policy large enough to cover your core goals, debt, and ongoing living expenses
- A will or living trust, depending on your situation
- An automatic withdraw from your general account into your different savings/investment accounts
- A debt repayment plan if you have any debt besides your mortgage
- A semi-annual assessment of your net worth, preferably with a financial advisor
- A plan for how you will share/tithe or give back to others
- An up-to-date estate plan if your net worth, including potential life insurance payouts is around $1 million or higher, for estate tax reasons.

Estate Planning

The final step in the creation of your financial plan is to establish an estate or succession plan. It often amazes us how people will work so hard to build wealth, and then lose it through the lack of long-term planning.

When creating your estate plan, certain things must be taken into consideration.

If you are self-employed, whether you're an independent contractor or own your own business, part of your estate plan should be a succession plan. A succession plan answers the following questions:

• Who will take over your business if you are unable to work or choose to close the business?
• To whom do you want to leave your estate, meaning all your assets?
• Do you want your estate broken up and divided among certain people?
• Do you want your business or hard-won assets to keep on living, or performing a job, even after you're no longer here?

If you find yourself asking where do I even start and do I really need to worry about estate planning? Well then rest assured, we have a great program that can help you answer that question. Just let us know.

By this point, you should have a strong enough foundation in place that you can start working on truly creating your wealth. Ideally, you have all of your debt paid off except for your mortgage, which has freed up a lot more disposable income. Hopefully, you also have a good understanding of your goals, dreams, and gift structures. When you are able to incorporate your gifts into your financial plan, things will start to go even more smoothly

With these basic foundational systems in place, the goal is to keep your investments growing, which in turn allows you to stay focused on your plan. You may want to also consider creating different gifting strategies, such as a charitable remainder trust. This is where you will be able to leave your mark on humanity. Now you can truly fulfill your life's purpose.

Andrew Carnegie, who is still considered one of the wealthiest men in the world though he died in 1919, set a goal that he was going to spend the first half of his life building a fortune and the second half giving it away. He then created the Carnegie Foundation, which has helped fund libraries, world peace, education, and scientific research. With the fortune he made from business, he built Carnegie Hall and has contributed millions of dollars to worthy causes. What are your goals for creating a legacy?

Congratulations! You made it!
You are truly on your way to becoming financial
independent!

"By ourselves we can do amazing things, yet together we can climb the highest mountains."
- Mike Raber

EPILOGUE

Mike

Throughout this book, Sabrina and I have shared our dreams. Without the help of Brian and Beverly Buffini , everyone at Buffini Company, many mentors along the way, we probably would not have been able to write this book. The creation of this dream has been a journey and has required the help of many people.

It's years. I know important to thank my wife, Jennifer, for staying on board all these it hasn't been easy for her, for it must have seemed that I simply floated from one idea to the next, even though I continued to move in an upward direction.

We would like to extend our sincere appreciation for the support and assistance we have received along the way. We are honored to call you our mentors and friends. We invite you, our reader, to join us on this journey. The dream and the future have merged wonderfully together. Together, let's change the world into the place it was designed to be! We hope that you have enjoyed this book, the many stories, and are putting into action your plan for becoming financially free. If we can do it, so can you! Through faith, anything is possible.

Sabrina

In the end, everything turned out the way I always dreamed it would. I got into the Philharmonic Orchestra after a brief period on wait list. Although I was devastated at first, I used the same tactics and same work ethic I learned in my business. I practiced harder than ever and sat in on all the rehearsals. As a result, I asked to join the orchestra and I was ecstatic. With more practice and another great year of orchestra rehearsals, I was lucky enough to get into the highest-level orchestra, and I played in that the last couple years I was in high school.

I was even able to be a part of the tour orchestra that traveled to Prague and Vienna, performed on incredible stages, and won second in an international competition. To this day, these events remain some of the best I have experienced part of who I have become.

As part of the Milwaukee Youth Symphony Orchestra, I was also given the opportunity to compose four pieces for ensembles in the program. I wrote a flute chorale piece, two string orchestra pieces, and most recently, a thirty-four-part symphonic piece, all in part because of the Milwaukee Youth Symphony Orchestra and the many musical things I learned as a member of it.

I could go on about the many other musical opportunities I was given because of my background, my business, and my orchestra, because they really have helped me this much. They taught me that no matter what your dreams are, no matter what path you want to pursue, whether it's a business about money or playing in the spotlight, if you work hard and put your mind to it, anything is possible.

Because of these events and all that I have learned with Children and Beyond, I am now leading a life doing what I love, helping people and performing. I was able to get into the Music school at The Ohio State University as a flute performance major.

From a young age, I was taught the value of serving in one's community and was fortunate to have been given opportunities to serve. I saw the impact that financial education had on my peers and was insistent on continuing to educate, inform, and better my community. As I grew older, that innate activism rose. In high school, I was a member of the National Honor Society, gathering volunteering hours from volunteering with the Milwaukee Youth Symphony Orchestra and other local organizations.

In my undergraduate degree, I made it a priority to help those around me by actively seeking out opportunities. After my freshman year at the Ohio State University, I took part in a two-month internship with the Milwaukee Youth Symphony Orchestra. While most of my work consisted of filling databases and developing marketing strategies, I was a fervent advocate for educational outreach, particularly involving musical literacy. The remainder of my time at Ohio State was spent on this new passion of music education for all.

When applying for graduate studies, I intentionally researched universities and communities that would further my work and passion for helping under resourced children. I eventually chose to attend the University of South Carolina School of Music, a flagship university in the world of music entrepreneurship.

Within my first semester of my master's degree, I discovered a need in the Columbia, South Carolina community for music education, particularly for under resourced children. Music education has long been proven to improve early cognitive development, foster confidence, and develop critical thinking skills in young students. However, many students do not have access to any music education. Several programs, notably El Sistema, have been created to provide music education for under-resourced students, however the cost to create such a program and purchase instruments is a deterrent. Through many discussions with my advisor, the Dean of the school, and other community partners, I decided to begin my own program. From this came Find Your Beat, a percussion ensemble arts education program that uses recycled products, such as buckets, pieces of wood, soda bottles, or other items found in the community. The program focuses as an after-school program for Columbia children in low income neighborhoods. Students learn basic musical principles such as rhythm, form, and time. Rehearsals are led in the Samba School style, a form of pedagogy that consists of the students being taught a repeating rhythm on their individual instrument.

In addition to rehearsals, there are also leadership classes and games, as well as design courses, where students can create their own instruments out of these recycled objects and compose their own music. The entire program is meant to be hands on, from the creation of the instruments, all the way to the performance of the pieces.

In December of 2018, Find Your Beat students performed at the Columbia Carillon Holiday parade. The children performed on a float for both live and televised audiences. This experience was incredible. To see the looks on my students' faces and to hear them exclaim their excitement was a highlight of my life, and I hope the performance was a highlight of theirs. Throughout the semester, my students improved greatly, and were mastering several musical tenets and proficient in other areas. I would frequently talk about the lesson experience with the students in order to gauge their feelings and saw an increase in self-confidence and musical ability. Their interest in school and overall leadership skills improved and many said that music was their favorite class. Students developed a strong emotional connection with myself and my partner instructor. Many of them began to confide in me, give me hugs, and cry when we left.

These benefits are not why am so passionate about teaching these incredible kids, but it is the odd student who tells me that they want to grow up to be a music teacher, who is excited to show me the new musical skill they practiced and learned, who teaches their younger sibling in class how to hold drumsticks but more so how to be a good human. I have seen firsthand the magic that comes from bringing music to a child that may not otherwise have that opportunity Basic music education can afford these children the opportunity to be more creative, happier, more productive, and have higher work ethics. It is my hope that Find Your Beat gives them something to be proud of that is truly theirs.

The possibilities for program expansion are plentiful. At its core, Find Your Beat would function well as a general music addition for current youth orchestras hoping to engage younger students. As a dream, Find Your Beat could be expanded city and even statewide. Eventually, it could be a national program. With the low costs of recycled materials and the benefits of music education, it is incredibly easy to recreate.

I consider myself lucky to have found a life calling that makes me so passionate, especially one that draws on so many important parts of my past. And while it is my goal to continue to affect the children in my neighborhood, both through financial and musical literacy, I also wish to affect my community through collaboration and compassion. As this book comes to an end, I invite you to join us as we work to create real change in our communities and make the world a better place, one bucket, one dollar, and one child at a time.

I hope that's what you take most from this book. Teaching your children, the same things I was taught and have been privileged to teach others, may be the key that unlocks their highest hopes, just like it was mine. Join me in changing our mindsets, the mindset of children, and the future of the world. Because that's what we can do: change the world, one child at a time.

Follow us at www.childrenandbeyond.com. Or check out even more stories and lessons at the Influencers Journey Pod Cast Show.

ADDITIONAL RESOURCES

Great web sites around personal, business, and financial growth:

www.childrenandbeyond.com
www.centsiblewealthsolutions.com
www.lighthousecourseacademy.com

www.ingramcontent.com/pod-product-compliance
Lightning Source LLC
LaVergne TN
LVHW011235080426
835509LV00005B/504